THE SPARTANS

L. F. Fitzhardinge

THE SPARTANS

WITH 150 ILLUSTRATIONS

THAMES AND HUDSON

Ancient Peoples and Places

GENERAL EDITOR: GLYN DANIEL

Library of Congress Catalog card number 79-66136

Filmset and printed in Great Britain by BAS Printers Limited, Over Wallop, Hampshire

Contents

Preface

My continuing interest in Sparta and the apparent contradictions in her history began with an undergraduate essay written many years ago for Christopher Cox at New College, Oxford. No opportunity for serious work on the subject presented itself until 1969, when, as a Commonwealth Fellow of St John's College, Cambridge, I was able to seek advice from various people on the project and to begin the systematic collection of material, which was virtually completed during another visit to Europe in 1975.

The work has been made enjoyable by the ready help and encouragement of many people, not all of whom can be listed here. I am especially grateful to J. A. Crook of St John's College, Cambridge, A. Andrewes of New College, Oxford, John Boardman of Wadham College, Oxford and A. H. McDonald, formerly of Clare College, Cambridge, and now of Perth, W. A. The two last added to my debt by reading and commenting on the draft, as did D. H. Kelly of Macquarie University, Sydney, and my wife. None of these are to be blamed for the result.

Most of the work was done in the libraries of the Australian National University and the University of Sydney, and outside Australia in those of the Hellenic Society, London, the Ashmolean Museum, Oxford, the Archaeological Museum of the University of Cambridge, and the British School at Athens. To all of these and to their staffs I offer my sincere thanks. This work was supplemented by time spent in the British Museum, the Louvre, the museums of Athens and Sparta, and the National Museum in Belgrade. I am grateful to Denys Haynes of the British Museum, R. V. Nicholls of the Fitzwilliam Museum, Cambridge, and M. Vickers of the Ashmolean Museum, Oxford, for help with objects in their care. B. B. Shefton of the University of Newcastle on Tyne gave a Saturday to discussion of the large bronze vessels, and H. W. Catling introduced me to the new excavations at the Menelaeum. Paul Cartledge kindly allowed me to use his thesis in the final revision of my work.

The sources of the illustrations are acknowledged in the List of Illustrations, and I am grateful to all those who provided photographs and gave me permission to use them. Special thanks are due to the German Archaeological Institute (DAI) in Athens, without the availability of whose splendid collection of photographs much of the work would have been impossible. I am also indebted to Mrs Christine Grishin for the trouble she took with the drawings, and to the Visual Aids Section of the ANU for help in copying material for my study.

Professor Glyn Daniel, General Editor of the Ancient Peoples and Places series, and the Editorial Board of Thames and Hudson greatly heartened me by their ready acceptance of the still unwritten book, and the publisher's editor has been patient and helpful while it was being written.

Finally I thank Mrs Morna Vellacott and Mrs Rosemary Rodwell for their kindness in typing the draft and Mrs Anne Clugston for her expert typing of the final version.

For classical names I have adopted the form familiar to English readers; for modern Greek place-names the transliteration used by the Permanent Committee on Geographical Names. For the former I have followed the *Oxford Classical Dictionary*, for the latter the Blue Guide. In the case of modern Greek authors I have used the form used by them when writing in English or French, e.g. Christou, not Khristou.

1
The Problem

For more than two thousand years, from the beginning of the fourth century BC to the early twentieth century AD, a clear and consistent idea of Sparta prevailed unquestioned. It has had a wide influence on European thought and has even passed into our language; we all know what is meant by a spartan meal or a laconic speech, and many who have never learnt ancient history have heard of the mother who bade her soldier son return with his shield or on it, or the boy who let the fox hidden in his cloak gnaw through to his heart rather than show his pain.

Sparta stood for the complete antithesis to Athens, with her brilliant culture, freedom-loving but fickle democracy and cult of the individual. According to one's point of view Sparta was a model of stability, order and discipline or of reaction, regimentation and repression. 'The organization of your state', Plato wrote, 'is that of an army camp, not of people who live in a town.'[1] Thucydides contrasted the material appearance of the two cities. A visitor in the distant future, he wrote, seeing only the ruins of Sparta, the scattered foundations of her houses and the absence of costly temples, would never believe that she had been one of the most powerful cities of Greece, while the splendid ruins of Athens would lead him to think she had been twice as great as she really had been.[2] As an early German visitor exclaimed: 'The arts and learning never flowered here.'[3]

Sparta, so the story ran, owed this character to an inspired lawgiver, Lycurgus, who at some uncertain but distant time had given her a constitution, a military organization and a set of social institutions, enforced by a system of education which controlled every male from seven to sixty. This made Sparta unique in Greece, and changed her from the worst to the best governed of Greek states. Everything about Lycurgus was obscure, his date, the source of his laws, even whether he was man or god, but all agreed on the antiquity and venerability of his laws and that to them Sparta owed both her character and her military greatness.

In the nineteenth century scraps of evidence were beginning to appear which did not fit into the accepted framework. The English traveller W. M. Leake noticed in 1805 that the whole site was covered with wrought stones, which were daily being broken up and carted off for building material. While he recognized that most of the visible remains, such as the theatre, were of late date, he rightly concluded that 'in every age those religious feelings which were founded on the common belief and customs of Greece, and which were gratified by the dedication of splendid edifices and works of sculpture, were as strong at Sparta as in any part of the country . . . Artists, therefore, could never have been without encouragement.'[4] Seventy years later his guess received confirmation from the building of a local museum into which the chance finds which were turning up in Sparta and its vicinity could be gathered, and the publication of its collection, including examples of the 'hero reliefs' on local marble, by two German scholars.[5]

Meanwhile, evidence of another kind came from Egypt, with the discovery in 1855 and publication in 1863 of a papyrus containing, albeit in mutilated form, a hundred lines of one of the 'maiden songs' or choruses for girls of Alcman, whose work had been hitherto known only from scraps quoted by later writers. Both the restoration of the text and its interpretation, however, were difficult, and little notice was taken of it by historians.

One of the very few exceptions was Professor J. P. Mahaffy, of Trinity College, Dublin. In his *History of Greek Literature* published in 1880 he pointed out the significance of the new fragment for the study of the Spartan society of the seventh century. Four years later a visit to the site of Sparta led him to question strongly the accepted view, with a remarkable anticipation of modern research. So far from being, as he had been brought up to believe, 'hardy mountaineers, living in a rude alpine country, with sterile soil', the Spartans, he saw, had occupied one of the richest and most fertile sites in Greece, and so 'must from the very outset of their career have had better food, better climate, and hence much more luxury than their neighbours'. Geography and archaeology pointed the same way as poetry:

> 'We are led to the same conclusion by the art-remains which are now coming to light . . . They show us that there was an archaic school of sculpture, which produced votive and funeral reliefs, and therefore that the old Spartans were by no

> means so opposed to art as they have been represented in the histories. The poetry of Alcman, with its social and moral freedom, its suggestions of luxury and good living, shows what kind of literature the Spartan rulers thought fit to import and encourage in the city of Lycurgus. The whole sketch of Spartan society which we read in Plutarch's *Life* and other late authorities seems rather to smack of imaginary reconstruction on Doric principles than of historical reality.'[6]

But Mahaffy did not follow this up, 'lest I should have all the pedants down on me', and his voice was unheeded. Nor was there yet enough evidence to support a serious challenge to the received doctrine, entrenched as it seemingly was behind a mass of detailed erudition. Since the pioneer modern work in three volumes of J. E. F. Manso at the beginning of the century, but especially in its second half, theses and inaugural addresses on Spartan history were produced in every country of Europe, especially in Germany. All worked and reworked the limited base of literary material, and none are now read, but their sheer mass served to smother new ideas.[7]

Then came the excavations at Sparta of the British School in the five years from 1906 to 1910. Before this the School had undertaken a topographical reconnaissance of Laconia and a catalogue of the collection already in the Sparta Museum, but beyond demonstrating the existence over a considerable span of time of a local school of sculpture, these gave little indication of what was to come. As the excavations progressed, a wealth of ivory carvings, bronzes, terracottas and painted pottery revealed a new Sparta, in the main stream of archaic Greek culture, in which the minor arts had flourished and foreign contacts had been numerous and fruitful. The material was supplemented by further excavations at Sparta from 1924 to 1928, by the British, and at Amyclae in 1926 by the German School.

The stylistic relation of the finds to one another and the fact that they formed an unbroken sequence from the Geometric period down to, and perhaps beyond, the sixth century proved their local origin and made it possible by analogy to identify as Laconian objects found elsewhere. In particular, the class of painted pottery long known from Etruscan graves and generally attributed to Cyrene were shown beyond doubt to be Spartan, and as more examples were discovered a wide network of exports covering most of the Mediterranean world was revealed.

This, then, is the Spartan paradox: on the one hand the rude, austere and narrow barrack depicted in the written sources; on the other the normal, creative and pleasure-loving society suggested by the new finds. How could these be reconciled, or, if they could not be reconciled, what credence was to be given to each type of source?

One of the first solutions to be proposed lay in the application of comparative anthropology (the influence of Sir James Frazer's *Golden Bough* was then at its height). This school was represented by M. P. Nilsson and H. Jeanmaire.[8] Starting from the evidence of continuous development from the earliest Dorian settlement, they rejected the traditional legislator, and saw in the distinctive Spartan institutions survivals of an early age long outgrown in most of Greece, for which analogies were found among the primitive tribes of Africa and Australia. Sparta represented a normal but arrested development, in which the customs of tribal times survived to be adapted to the different social needs of historical Sparta long after their original significance had been forgotten. The age-groups, the common mess and the *crypteia*[9] were all shown to have convincing analogies in primitive custom.

Others, including the excavators themselves, preferred to retain as much of the literary tradition as possible, but to bring the 'revolution' down from the eighth or ninth century to correspond with a sharp cultural break of which they saw evidence in the finds, variously placed at the beginning or in the middle of the sixth century, and associated either with the second Messenian war or with the mysterious ephor Chilon, whose reputation as one of the seven sages seemed out of proportion to anything recorded of him.

In 1925 this latter approach received the strong and persuasive support of the two greatest Greek historians of that generation. In his chapter in volume III of the *Cambridge Ancient History* H. T. Wade-Gery saw the *Eunomia* as a direct result of the Messenian war and at the same time as 'a sort of inoculation against democracy' which was beginning to undermine the archaic aristocracies elsewhere in Greece. Its date he put in the last years of the seventh century, a date which he found supported by oblique hints in the literature and the 'conclusive evidence' of the excavations for a sudden and drastic change in Spartan life at that time. In the same year V. Ehrenberg in his *Neugründer des Staates* compared the constitutional changes at Sparta with those taking place at Athens during the sixth century, and assigned them to a date about 550, associating the change with the successful conclusion of the war with Tegea and the formation of the Peloponnesian League and attributing it to Chilon. He too supported his date by reference to the archaeological material as well as to the general context of political development in Greece. G. Glotz in France, in the same year, adopted the hypothesis of a radical change about 600, and his perception of the fictional element in Spartan history, 'le roman spartiate' was not pressed to its logical conclusion.

Four years later Ehrenberg enshrined his version in the article on Sparta in the *Realenzyklopädie* of Paully-Wissowa, and the combined weight of these authorities carried the day. When the official publication of the excavations, *Artemis Orthia*, appeared in 1929, it proved disappointing. In the twenty years since the excavations, the authors had smoothed out in their own minds the doubts and inconsistencies of the preliminary reports to favour the theory of a sharp cultural break, and presented altogether too bland a surface. Their chronology was seriously questioned, especially in a detailed review by E. Kunze in *Gnomon* in 1933, and they reacted to criticism with a fierce defensiveness which inhibited further discussion, especially as the material was mostly not at that time available for re-examination.

A new and important contribution was made in 1934 by a French scholar, F. Ollier, in a book in which he demonstrated in great detail that the traditional account of Spartan history was substantially a fiction, a 'mirage', fabricated in Sparta for internal political use, then exported as an adjunct to Spartan diplomacy and in the fourth century taken up and embellished as a source of oligarchic propaganda and philosophic model building. All writing on Sparta later than 400 BC is, Ollier showed, tainted by the 'mirage' and, at best, suspect.

In a short review of Ollier in 1935, A. A. Blakeway pointed in another direction. He demonstrated that the finds did not in fact show a sudden break, and suggested that the cause of Sparta's cultural decline was economic, not political. Yet another course was taken in 1938 by A. Andrewes in what was to be the first of a valuable series of papers in which, accepting Wade-Gery's date for the reforms, he turned back to a close re-examination of the literary sources, and especially of the enigmatic 'Great Rhetra' preserved by Plutarch, a pursuit in which after the war he was joined by Wade-Gery and Ehrenberg. But this, for all the scholarship and acumen it called forth, proved a red herring.

Since 1945 there has been no slackening of interest in Sparta. Eight general books have been published in English alone, as well as numerous articles and special studies. There have been two books in French and at least one in German, while in Italian P. Ianni has produced two volumes of stimulating studies of Spartan literary culture. Each of these has its own merits and insights, but none is wholly satisfactory. This is perhaps partly because, as one critic has said, they try to find answers to questions to which there is no answer, but partly also because they all, in varying degrees, take as their starting point the traditional sources and try to fit the archaeological evidence into this framework. In this book I have tried to reverse this procedure; to survey first the contemporary evidence, and only then to see how far the later sources are consistent with it.

Recently, fresh synthetic studies of sections of the archaeological material have made it more easily accessible. The pioneer works of E. Langlotz (1927) and E. A. Lane (1934) had for some time no successors, though the publication of new material and articles on single items, notably those of E. Kunze on successive bronzes from Olympia, continued. B. B. Shefton in 1954 and P. Pelagatti in 1957 carried much further Lane's work in the recognition of the work of individual vase painters and in fixing the chronology of Laconian pottery. A new stage began with the publication by J. Boardman of a short article which, while broadly vindicating the stratigraphy of the original excavators, proposed for the first time an acceptable scheme of chronology. Since then, very full monographs have been devoted to the ivories by E. L. H. Marangou in 1969 and to the sixth-century vase painters by C. M. Stibbe in 1972. At the same time the display of the Sparta museum has been improved and extended, and the pioneer guide published by C. Christou in 1960 has been followed, while this book was being written, by the excellent handbook of G. Steinhauer in 1976. Lately, too, the archaeological material for the early period, including much from the storerooms of the Sparta Museum, has been examined in detail by P. Cartledge in a thesis as yet unpublished.

2
The Setting

Sparta stood, like its modern namesake, at the head of an inland alluvial plain where the river Eurotas emerges from the Arcadian mountains, about 200 m (650 ft) above sea level. On the north the hills approach the town and a low spur projects into it to form its acropolis. On its eastern side the river flows in a wide sandy bed overgrown with reeds and oleander between high banks. Easily fordable in summer, in winter it becomes a raging torrent, subject to violent floods like that which destroyed the older temple of Artemis Orthia in the first half of the sixth century BC.

The town, irregular in shape, sprawled over a group of low hills on the right bank, with a circuit of 9.5 km (6 miles). Here, in four suburbs or 'villages', with Amyclae 6 km (4 miles) to the south as a fifth, the Spartans had their houses and gardens; the fact that here, as nowhere else in Greece, burials were allowed inside the town shows that there was no overcrowding. There was no town centre. In the north-eastern part the temple of Athena of the Bronze House and one or two other temples stood on the 'acropolis', itself little more than a hummock and unfortified. On the level ground at its foot was a retail market of sorts, the meeting place of the Council, and from the fifth century a portico built from the spoils of the Persian wars and memorials to Leonidas and Pausanias. Other shrines and monuments and the family tombs of the two royal houses were distributed through the town. The most important temple, that
of Artemis Orthia, was out of sight down by the river; the most 5
conspicuous, the shrine of Menelaus and Helen, was outside the 4, 2
town altogether on a high bluff on the other bank. Another important cult-centre, the shrine of Apollo Hyacinthus, the Amyclaeum, was out in the country near Amyclae. To the ordinary Greek the town looked more like a cluster of rural villages than a city.

The soil of the plain is very fertile, though stones washed down through the centuries from the flanks of Taygetus make it

1 Sparta and Taygetus, *c.* 1910

hard to cultivate and better suited to fruit trees and vines than to grain. By Greek standards it is unusually well watered with streams from Taygetus and perennial springs along its foot. Modern travellers have always been impressed by the luxuriant beauty of the site, standing out with its groves of oranges and olives like an oasis. The summers, though tempered by evening breezes from Taygetus, are somewhat hotter than near the coast and the winters colder. Frosts are not uncommon, and there is some snow; on parts of Taygetus just a few miles to the west snow lies almost all the year. The rainfall, 817 mm (33 in.), almost all in winter, is more than twice that of Athens. A geological fault runs near by, and throughout its history the town has intermittently suffered severe earthquakes.

Though fertile, the plain is small and sharply defined, its greatest length being about 14 km (9 miles) and its breadth 5 km (3 miles). To the west rises the Taygetus range, its rocky crags seamed with deep gorges, shutting out the sun a good hour before its setting. The highest peak of the chain, Mt Ilias, of 2407 m (7874 ft), is opposite the southern end of the plain. Halfway up is a level terrace, thickly wooded in ancient times, a

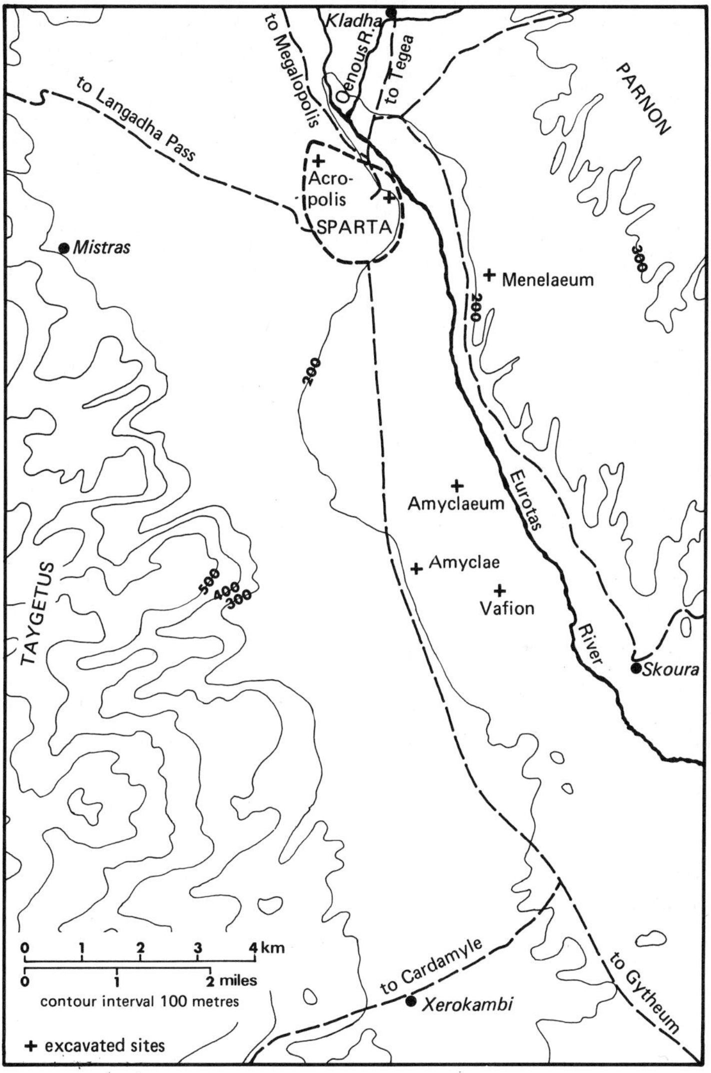

2 The Vale of Sparta

haunt of wild beasts and a favourite hunting ground. On the east side, the Parnon range drops into the river bed in a line of picturesque red hills. Towards the south the plain is bisected by a low ridge on which Amyclae stood, dividing the vale of Sparta from its southern extension. At its southern end the plain is terminated by the edge of the Vardunochoria plateau, which projects from the foot of Taygetus and confines the river to a narrow gorge from which it emerges in a series of low falls some 40 km (25 miles) further down into the plain of Helos, larger and no less fertile than that of Sparta but in ancient times notoriously marshy and fever-ridden.

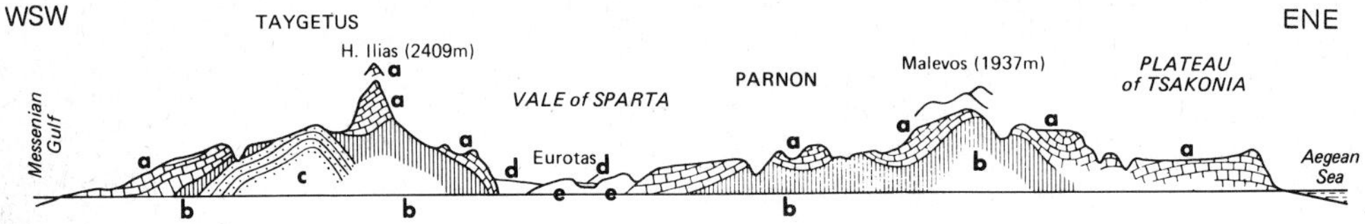

3 Section of Laconia through Sparta. Scale of distance 1:600,000; of height, 1:200,000. (*a*) Tripolis limestone; (*b*) Crystalline schist; (*c*) Crystalline limestone; (*d*) Alluvial soil; (*e*) Pleistocene marl

The territory naturally dominated by Sparta comprised the whole basin of the Eurotas between Taygetus and Parnon and down to the Laconian gulf. This was Lacedaemon, or Laconia proper. On the north it was bounded by the tangled hill country where Taygetus, the Arcadian highlands and Parnon meet, with ill-defined watersheds and barren, stony slopes, except on its western edge where a comparatively easy route leads between Taygetus and the Eurotas up to the plain of Megalopolis. This was the Sciritis, a land of tough highlanders, Arcadian by race but early absorbed into the Laconian state and accorded a special place in its army.

To the east, the valley is divided from the Aegean coast by the broad mass of Parnon, a barrier less spectacular but hardly less effective than that of Taygetus. A high plateau of limestone, waterless and deeply eroded, even now no road crosses its central portion. The highest point is at the northern end toward the Argolid, where it rises to 1935 m (6354 ft); opposite Sparta it reaches 1839 m (6000 ft). From here a series of parallel ridges without conspicuous peaks runs south-east, maintaining a height of 1000 to 1200 m (3000 to 4000 ft), and reaching the sea above Epidaurus Limera. On the Aegean side a plateau about 800 m (2500 ft) high, wide in the north and narrowing to the south, drops to the sea in a line of inhospitable cliffs, broken occasionally by a deep ravine at the mouth of which a patch of arable land supports a small village. This was the region of Cynuria, forming no part of Laconia proper – from which even today it is largely isolated – but part of the Aegean world, a fact symbolized by the reputed Ionian origin of its people. At its northern and more accessible end it marched with the Argolid, and until the sixth century the whole of it, together with the island of Cythera, was controlled by Argos, the nearest maritime power.

On the west the forested peaks of Taygetus towered above the valley along its whole length. A low saddle at the head of the Laconian gulf afforded easy access from Gytheum to Oetylus on the Messenian gulf, and separated the main range from its continuation in the rugged and inaccessible mountains of the

Taenarum peninsula, the medieval and modern Maina. Before 1940 no road crossed Taygetus, and the few tracks were difficult for the most active traveller, and impassable in winter. The route most used in modern times, across the Langadha pass round the north of Mt Ilias, seems not to have been used in antiquity, and the only route to the plain of Messenia was the one round the end of the range; a very difficult track led from the southern end of the Spartan plain round the southern flank of Mt Ilias to Kardamyle on the Messenian gulf.

4 The Menelaeum in 1910

6, 2

Within these boundaries the river, with its narrow ribbon of alluvial soil between high banks, impedes rather than assists communication. From its right bank the 500 m (1600 ft) plateau of Vardunochoria runs back to Taygetus. Waterless except along its western edge, it drops steeply to the gulf above Gytheum. On the left bank a somewhat similar plateau fringes Parnon, eroded into foothills as it approaches the river. For the most part this is arid and scrub-covered, but some olives grow on the lower slopes and here and there a pocket of better soil supports a village, the most important being Yeraki, the ancient Geronthrae. Here a high and difficult route leads over Parnon past Kosmas to Leonidhion (ancient Prasiae). This was the only direct access to the Aegean coast between the road to Astros round the north of

2, 3

Parnon and the head of the Laconian gulf, where the dry plain of Molaoi gave access to a fairly low route across to Epidauros Limera, just north of Monemvasia.

Though wheat land was very scarce – the staple grain was always barley – and much of its large area consisted of rugged mountain or waterless limestone, Laconia was not an especially poor country. The uplands afforded extensive sheepwalks, and olives could be grown on their lower slopes. Taygetus provided timber and game, and the springs along its foot watered orchards and vineyards. Marble was plentiful, though the best kinds were not exploited till Roman times. Gold and silver and, more important, copper and tin for bronze, were lacking, but iron was mined and also probably lead. The shellfish that produced the prized purple dye were abundant in the Laconian gulf; this had perhaps once drawn Phoenician traders to Gytheum, and later the dye was used for the cloaks of Spartan soldiers.

When Sparta first entered the realm of history, however tentatively, she already controlled the whole Eurotas watershed and her subjects had spread from Gytheum to the Messenian gulf and were pasturing their herds on the western slopes of Taygetus. There was no other centre that could dispute the dominion of the holders of the rich land of the plain, and

5 Site of the temple of Orthia today

6 The Langadha pass, from an old photograph

nowhere where one could arise. Such a region did not lend itself to the normal development of a Greek city-state. There was no way in which its far-flung inhabitants could meet to share in its government, nor could their communities stand on their own. The special combination of subordination to the centre with local autonomy of the 'dwellers around' (*perioeci*) was imposed by geography; it was the natural outcome of the economic, and therefore military ascendancy of those who had secured the rich land of the plain over those who had been forced to seek land further out on the marginal 'frontier'.

Sparta not only monopolized the best land, but she stood at the meeting of the main routes that linked Laconia to the world beyond.

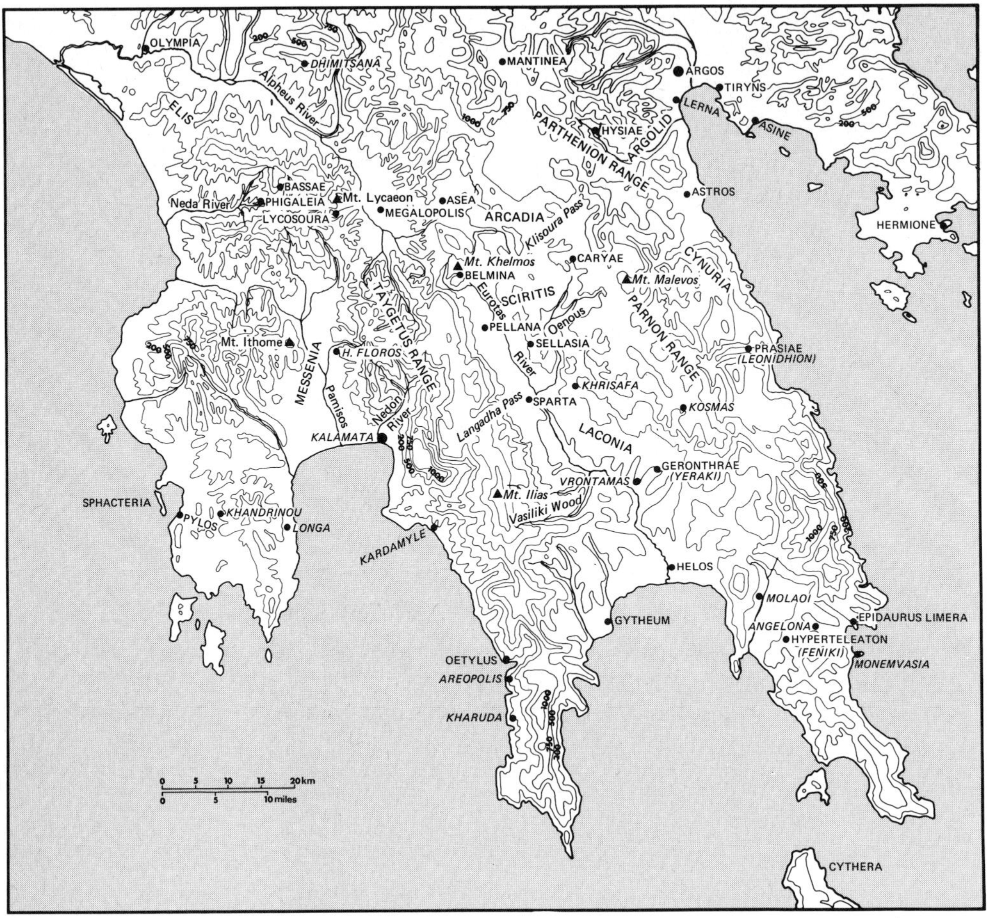

7 The southern Peloponnese

From very early times Gytheum had provided some contact with the Aegean and the eastern Mediterranean. Its harbour was small and it had no immediate hinterland to support a town, but depended on the easy though tedious road across Vardunochoria to Sparta a considerable distance inland. The purple dye of the *murex*, however, had attracted Phoenician and Syrian traders. Hence too ran the direct sea route to Crete and to Cyrene in north Africa, as well as the route by way of the Aegean islands to the west coast of Asia Minor. When Greek trade with the west developed, Gytheum was the nearest port for ships battered in rounding the notorious Cape Malea to rest and refit before launching into the open sea. As the wealth of Laconia grew it became a centre where eastern products were exchanged for wool and wine and oil, and later, pottery and bronzes.

The most important link with mainland Greece followed approximately the route of the modern road from Sparta to Tripolitsa. Crossing the Eurotas near the town, it followed the valley of the Oenous north for a few miles before climbing steeply onto a spur of Parnon and traversing some 30 km (19 miles) of lonely rock and scrub to descend by the Klisoura pass 930 m (3061 ft) above sea level to the high plain of Tegea, whence relatively easy routes lead to Argos and Corinth. About halfway a road branched to the right past Caryae and round the end of Parnon to Astros on the gulf of Argos. Though long and rough and at times steep this route is nowhere really difficult.

Another route, more important in ancient than in modern times, ran above the Eurotas north-west to Mt Khelmos and the frontier post of Belmina and down to the plain later occupied by Megalopolis, but until the fourth century without any political centre. Here within a few miles are the sources of the three largest rivers of the Peloponnese, the Eurotas, the Alpheus and the Pamisos. The Eurotas provided an easy route up from Sparta; the Alpheus led north-west to Olympia and Elis, while the Pamisos led by an easy descent into the plains of Messenia.

The geographical position of Sparta was thus very different from that of any other Greek city of comparable importance. Its inhabitants stood near the sea and within sight, or at most a few hours' march, of potentially hostile neighbours from whom they were separated by clear-cut natural boundaries; Sparta was 46 km (28 miles) from her only port at Gytheum and 57 km (36 miles) from her nearest independent neighbour, Tegea, to the north. Between Sparta and Tegea, and Sparta and Argos to the north-east there was no clearly defined frontier, but a broad wilderness of tangled and sparsely populated hills. It was the distance of her enemies, not the valour of her soldiers, that allowed Sparta to remain unwalled until the fourth century. But though remote, Sparta was not isolated, and throughout her history she was open to influences both from mainland Greece and from Ionia and the Levant.

3
The Pottery

We will begin our examination of the archaeological material with the pottery, which, since it is found in the greatest quantity in all levels of the excavation of any ancient site, forms the basis of the chronology and provides a framework to which objects of any other kind can be related.

In Mycenaean times Laconia seems to have been well populated and prosperous. More than thirty settlements are known from surface remains, though few have been excavated, and all tell the same story. At the end of the period known as Late Helladic (LH) about 1200 BC, whether as a result of war, pestilence or famine we do not know, this civilization came to an abrupt end. Whereas LH IIIB sherds are plentiful, those of LH IIIC are almost non-existent. A few survivors returned to squat among the ruins of their old homes, and then apparently dispersed among the rocks and hills. Other refugees formed a settlement at Epidaurus Limera on the Aegean, whence by degrees they emigrated to Cyprus and Asia Minor. The cult at the shrine near Amyclae was kept alive in an impoverished form through LH IIIC and the succeeding degenerate Submycenaean period almost, if not quite, until new settlers arrived to take it over, but for a century and a half or two centuries the evidence suggests that the area was virtually without people and certainly without any organized community. When the valley was settled again, the newcomers used a completely different type of pottery and generally, as at Sparta, chose new sites for their settlements, though possibly taking over some survivals of the old religion.[1]

The new pottery was of the family called Protogeometric, which had evolved a century or so earlier in Attica or central Greece from the remnants of the Submycenaean, but of a distinctive type with tenuous links with the west and north-west rather than with Argos or Athens. That many of the sherds by which the style is known are from the Amyclaeum is clearly due to chance; it shows no continuity with the local Sub-

8 Dancers with lyre; late Geometric fragment from Amyclae. Ht 22 cm

mycenaean, even though found in proximity with it, and the same style is found at Sparta itself and elsewhere in Laconia. Whether the newcomers brought the style with them or developed it after arriving we do not know, nor when it began, but it ended about the middle of the eighth century, and may perhaps have lasted for as much as two centuries. Throughout this time the style shows little change and no outside influence, suggesting an isolated people wholly absorbed in the arduous task of pioneering the resettlement of the long-desolate countryside.

The end of isolation was marked by the adoption from the north of the Geometric style, in a stage corresponding to the late Geometric of Argos and Corinth, about 750. The Spartan potters retained their own shapes and modified the new style in their own way. The result, competent rather than imaginative, became the third Geometric style of the Peloponnese, and was

9 Geometric fragment from Amyclae

sometimes exported to near neighbours as well as to Tarentum, where Sparta founded a colony at the end of the eighth century. Figures were seldom attempted, though occasionally scenes of human activity were copied from Argive pottery or horses and water birds from Corinthian. The style lasted for about a century with little change, giving the impression of a craft no longer isolated from its neighbours, but conservative and catering for a local and artistically undemanding market. For those who sought something more exciting, Protocorinthian began to be imported.

By 650 this was changing and a period of modest experiment was beginning. The most distinctive fabric of this period was the 'fine ware' used only for small vases of high quality. These are well shaped, with extremely thin walls imitating metal. The decoration is uniformly simple, consisting of a band of black and white squares between two rows of dots round the top, bands of varying thickness, purple as well as black, round the body of the vase and pointed rays rising in a circle from its foot. This was the Spartan reaction to the exuberance of the orientalizing styles coming into vogue elsewhere. It was perhaps the work of a single potter, and for a generation it almost monopolized dedications at the Spartan shrines, along with Protocorinthian.

For this reason, less is known of the larger and coarser vases of this period. On these, geometrical elements were grouped in new

10 Late Geometric fragments from the Amyclaeum

11 Head of a warrior wearing a conical helmet. Late Geometric fragment from the acropolis. Ht 6 cm

combinations, often in panels to produce alternate dark and light areas instead of covering the surface evenly as in Geometric. Human figures are rare. Perhaps the earliest is the thumbnail sketch of a head, still close to Geometric, from the Amyclaeum. 10
Slightly later is the very oriental-looking head from the acropolis, wearing a pointed helmet and with features recalling 11
the earliest ivory reliefs. The only other head is quite different in style and comes from the end of the period, about 630. It is a profile in outline of a woman with dark hair, set between panels of 'windmill sail' pattern on a large cup from the Orthia site, the neck of which was decorated with frontal relief heads in the middle Daedalic style. The head resembles the 'Melian' style of the Cyclades. Animals, heraldic lions, bulls and goats drawn in crude but lively outline and silhouette, with large, blobby heads,

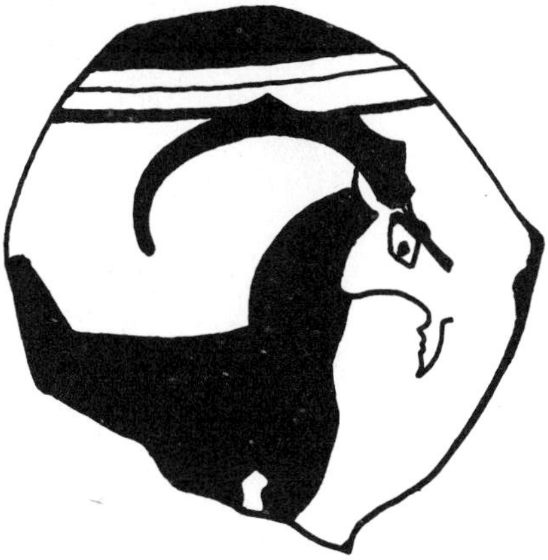

12 Ibex; Laconian I fragment from the Menelaeum. Ht 3 cm

are more common. These resemble the 'Wild Goat' style of Samos and Rhodes.

In the last quarter of the century, perhaps as a result of the introduction of the 'ripe' Corinthian style, Spartan taste in pottery underwent a change. Simple pots were still made, and would eventually reassert their influence, but most became extremely ornate, drawing for small pots as well as large on the combinations of 'Subgeometric' patterns developed on the larger shapes in the preceding period, reinforced by borrowings from Corinthian and new inventions. Large vases were now again dedicated as well as small. In addition to geometric patterns, while vegetable motives are rare, single or more rarely double, and once triple, friezes of animals are common, now of Corinthian rather than East Greek ancestry. Silhouette is modified by incision, at first hesitatingly and clumsily, but gradually more fluently, and purple is used for such details as the manes of lions and the tails of water birds. Gorgon heads are drawn, always in outline, and there is a fantastic creature, half bird, half panther. Figures, however, are always a subordinate part of the ornament, confined to friezes of a single species moving in the same direction.

The new style successfully held the home market against Corinthian, importation of which became rare compared with that of Protocorinthian earlier. Now too the export of Spartan pottery began in earnest. Only one example of Laconian I has been found outside Laconia, in Samos. Laconian II reached not only Samos and Sparta's colony at Tarentum, but Delos, Ephesus and Rhodes in the Aegean, Naucratis and Tauchira in Africa, and Caere in Etruria.

Closely related to the decoration of Laconian II vases was that of a particular type of terracotta ornament which, with its accompanying ridge caps and guttering, adorned and decorated the new temples being built in Sparta as elsewhere in Greece towards the end of the seventh century. This took the form of a semicircular disk, 1.5 m (5 ft) or more in diameter, fastened to the point of the gable, and brightly painted with concentric bands of various patterns arranged in a more or less standard order. Most of the known fragments come from Laconia and Messenia, many of them from Sparta itself, where the old temple of Orthia and the temple of Athena on the Acropolis, among others, were so adorned. Material and technique, as well as provenance, point to Sparta as the place of their invention and production, but they were also exported, for example to Bassae and to Aegina. The

13 Cup from Tarentum. Ht 9·5 cm; diam. 20 cm

finest and largest specimen was on the temple of Hera at Olympia, built about 600. In Laconia, they remained in use until they were superseded by marble reliefs of the same shape in the second half of the sixth century, and these continued in the characteristic Laconian marble down to the end of the fifth century, and in a less characteristically native form, till the first century BC.

The purely decorative style of vase painting reached its peak in the first quarter of the sixth century in the work of a painter known to us by three vases found in the same grave at Tarentum. The decoration of the outside is the same in all three, a superb procession of water birds with a band of black and white squares between two rows of dots round the rim and pointed rays rising from the base. The inside of one is plain black. In the other two
13 the bowl is filled by a ring of fish swimming round a central rosette; in one, called by Sir John Beazley the finest of all Laconian vases, the fish are in turn surrounded by dolphins. In some ways anticipating the next style though not belonging to it, these cups stand by themselves as the work of an individual of genius.

Laconian III began about 575, a few years before the flood which destroyed the old temple of Orthia.[2] Where Laconian II had been concerned only with decoration and had depended for its figures on outline and silhouette with only secondary use of incision, Laconian III was primarily interested in human subjects and in telling a story, using the true black-figure technique developed at Athens in the previous generation and later adopted at Corinth. Ornament, though still important, is subordinated to the main picture, and consists largely of arrangements of a limited number of highly stylized elements of vegetable origin, especially pomegranates and lotus buds. Animals and monsters are frequent and varied, whether participating in the main scene, as friezes or singly, and are now of Corinthian rather than East Greek derivation; empty spaces are filled with realistic domestic fowls. The figures are painted in black on a creamy yellow slip, with detail elaborately drawn by incision, and lavish use of purple often gives an effect of colour. Though inspired in the first place and always influenced by contemporary Corinthian and Attic, the Laconian painters were never merely imitators, and their work has a strongly marked character of its own.

The introduction of the new style may well have been the work of one man, possibly trained as a designer for ivory carvings or terracotta reliefs, both of which have close affinities with it. He was soon joined by others, but there seem never to have been more than a very small number of principal artists involved. Whilst the conventional division at 550 is in some ways convenient, there is no clear break between the work of the older and younger men, though there is a tendency towards a freer and less formal line and more fantastic subjects in later work, and one late minor painter reverts to a sort of pastiche of the earlier style. When the second generation stopped working about 525 they left no successors. The style was carried on for a few years longer, perhaps by journeymen from the disbanded workshops. Then came an abrupt decline, both technical and artistic, and though painted pottery was still produced at Sparta for the home market it is without quality or interest, consisting mostly of poor imitations of the all-conquering Attic. The same fate had overtaken Corinthian earlier, and the causes were clearly artistic and commercial, not political or social.

Almost from the beginning, vases in the new style were widely exported, and of the known examples, whole or fragmentary, far more were found outside Greece proper than at Sparta. The chances of preservation and discovery play a large part; most of our whole vases, for example, survived because of their use as grave furniture by the Etruscans. Stibbe lists only forty-five items with recognizable figures from Sparta itself (including Amyclae), yet over 2000 stems and feet of cups or dishes were unearthed in a single deposit at the shrine of Agamemnon and Cassandra at Amyclae.[3] In Greece itself, the greatest number come from Olympia, while others come from various sites in the northern Peloponnese and central Greece. Of the eighty per cent of Stibbe's catalogue found outside Greece, a third are from Samos and a sixth from Etruria. The rest come from sites in most parts of the Greek world and a few beyond, from Massilia and Carthage to Naucratis and Gordium. They are widespread in Sicily but less so in Greek southern Italy except for Tarentum, and though common in the south-eastern Aegean and north Africa they are rare in the north Aegean, where a find at Neapolis (Kavalla) in Thrace seems to belong to a single cargo, and absent from the Black Sea.

The high proportion of exports among the known vases exaggerates the importance of the wine cup (*kylix*), for although also popular at Sparta this shape had a special place in the export market, being the only Laconian ware found at many places which drew the rest of their crockery from elsewhere. From

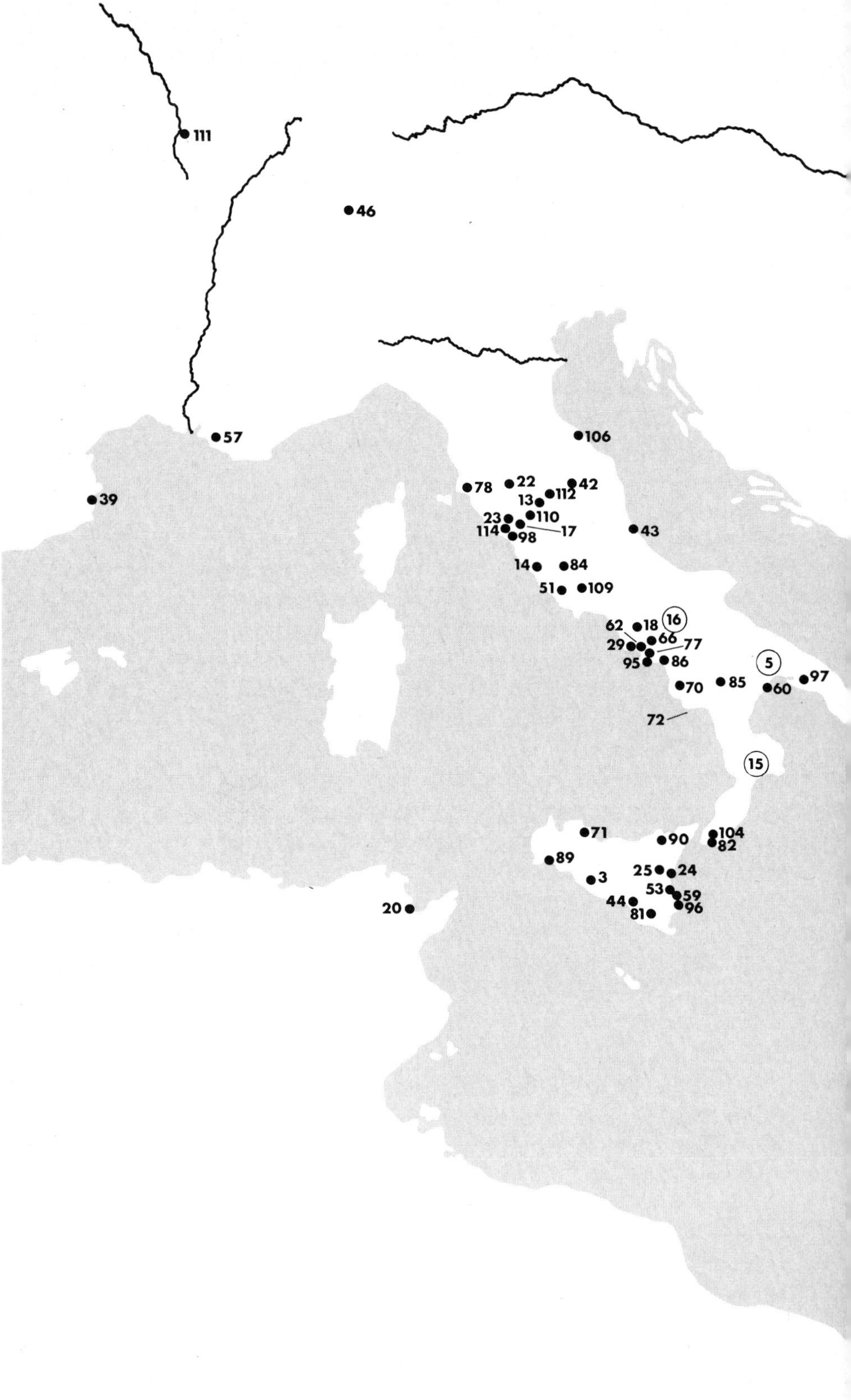

111
46
57
106
39
78
22
42
13
112
23
110
114
98
17
43
14
84
51
109
16
62
18
66
29
77
95
86
5
97
70
85
60
72
15
71
90
104
82
89
25
24
3
53
59
44
96
81
20

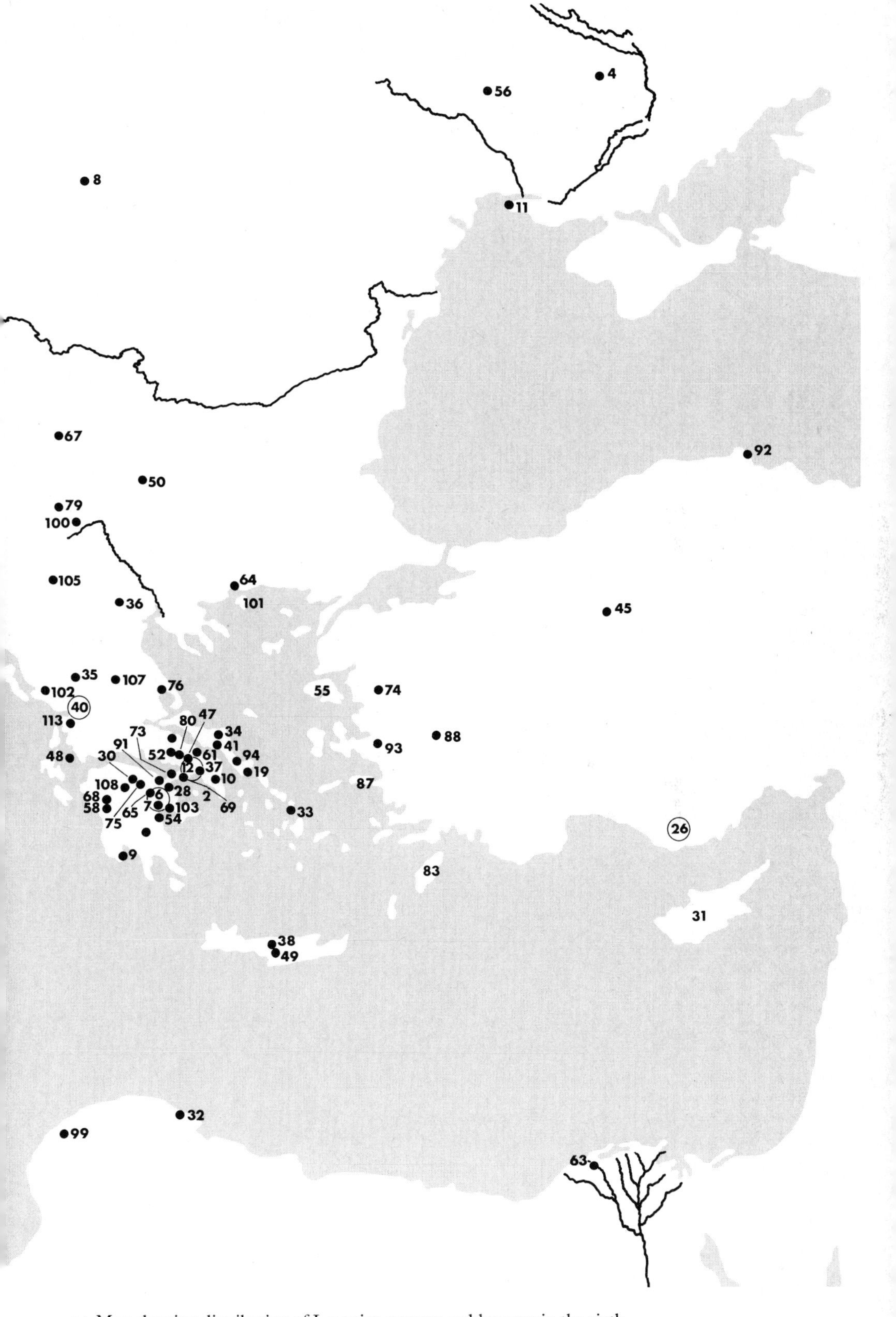

14 Map showing distribution of Laconian pottery and bronzes in the sixth century. (For key see overleaf)

Find-sites of Laconian Vases and Bronzes

KEY TO ILL. 14

Modern names in italics. a. decorated pottery; b. plain pottery; c. bronze statuettes; d. mirrors; e. large vessels and tripods.

1 *Aden Protectorate* (South Yemen). c
2 Aegina, central Greece. a, b
3 Agrigentum, Sicily. b
Ampurias, see Emporiae
4 *Annouka*, Ukraine. d
5 Apulia, southern Italy. b
6 Argive Heraeum, N.E. Peloponnese. b
7 Argos, N.E. Peloponnese. a, d.
8 *Artand*, Hungary. e
9 Asine, N. E. Peloponnese. b
10 Athens, central Greece. a, b, c, e
11 Berezan, Ukraine. b
Bisenzio, see Visentium.
12 Boeotia, central Greece. a
13 *Bolsena*, central Italy. b.
14 Caere (*Cerveteri*) central Italy. a, b
15 Calabria, S. Italy. b
16 Campania, S. Italy. e
17 *Canino*, central Italy. a
18 Capua, S. Italy. a
19 Carystus, central Greece. b
20 Carthage, N. Africa. a
21 *Castel Campanile*, central Italy. a
22 *Castellina*, central Italy. a
23 *Castro Farnese*, S. Italy. b
24 Catania, Sicily. a
25 Centuripae, Sicily. b
Cerveteri, see Caere.
26 Cilicia, Asia Minor. e
27 Corcyra, N.W. Greece. b
28 Corinth, central Greece. a, e
29 Cumae, S. Italy. a, b, e
30 Cynaetha (Kalavrita), N.W. Peloponnese, d
31 Cyprus, E. Mediterranean. d
32 Cyrene, N. Africa. a, e
33 Delos, Aegean sea. a, b
34 Delphi, central Greece. a, b, c, e
35 Dodona, N.W. Greece. c, e
36 Edessa, Macedonia. e
37 Eleusis, central Greece. c
38 Eleutherna, Crete. b
39 Emporiae (Ampurias), Spain. b
40 Epirus, N.W. Greece. e
41 Eretria, central Greece. e
42 *Foligno*, central Italy. e
43 *Francavilla Maritima*, central Italy. a
44 Gela, Sicily. a
45 Gordium, Asia Minor. a
46 *Grächuvil*, Switzerland. e
47 Haliartus, central Greece. a
48 Ithaca, N.W. Greece. a
49 Ida, Mt., Crete. e
50 *Janjevo*, Yugoslavia. e
Kalavryta, see Cynaetha
Kavalla, see Neapolis
51 Lavinium (*Pratica di Mare*), central Italy. a
52 Lebadea, central Greece. e
53 Leontini, Sicily. b
54 Lerna, N.E. Peloponnese. b
55 Lesbos, Aegean sea. b
56 *Martonosha*, Ukraine. e
57 Massilia, S. France. a, b
58 *Mazi*, N.W. Peloponnese. d
59 Megara Hyblaea, Sicily. a, b
60 Metapontum, S. Italy. e
61 Mycalessus (*Ritsona*), central Greece. b
62 Naples, S. Italy. a
63 Naucratis, Egypt. a, b
64 Neapolis (*Kavalla*), N.E. Greece. a
65 Nemea, N. E. Peloponnese. d
66 Nola, S. Italy. a
67 *Novi Pazar*, Yugoslavia. e
68 Olympia, N.W. Peloponnese. a, b, c, e
Orvieto, See Volsinii
69 Pagae, central Greece. b
70 Paestum, S Italy. e
71 *Palermo*, Sicily. b
72 Palinurus, cape, S. Italy. b
73 Perachora, central Greece. a, b
74 Pergamum, Asia Minor. a
Pesaro, see Treia
75 Pheneus, N. Peloponnese. c
76 Pherae (*Velastinon*), N. E. Greece. d
77 Pompeii, S. Italy. a
78 Populonia, central Italy. b
Pratica di Mare, see Lavinium
79 *Prizren*, Yugoslavia. e
80 Ptoion, central Greece. c
81 Ragusa, Sicily. b
82 Rhegium, S. Italy. b
83 Rhodes, Aegean sea. a, b
Ritsona, see Mycalessus
84 Rome, central Italy. a, b
85 *Sala Consilina*, S. Italy. e
86 Salernum, S. Italy. b
87 Samos, Aegean sea. a, b, c
88 Sardis, Asia Minor. a
89 Selinus, Sicily. a
90 *Serra Orlando*, Sicily. b
91 Sicyon, N. Peloponnese. a
92 Sinope, Black Sea. b
93 Smyrna, Asia Minor. a, b
94 Styra, central Greece. c
95 Surrentum (*Sorrento*), S. Italy. a
96 Syracuse, Sicily. a, b, d, e
97 Tarentum, S. Italy. a, b
98 Tarquinia, central Italy. a, b
99 Tauchira (*Tocra*), N. Africa. a
100 *Tetovo*, Yugoslavia. e
101 Thasos, Aegean sea. b
102 Thesprotia, N.W. Greece. e
103 Tiryns, N.E. Peloponnese. b
Tocra, see Tauchira
104 *Torre Galli*, S. Italy. b
105 *Trebenište*, Yugoslavia. e
106 Treia (*Pesaro*), central Italy. e
107 Trikke (*Trikkala*), N.E. Greece. e
108 Tripotama, N.W. Peloponnese. e
Velestinon, see Pherae
109 Velitrae, central Italy. a
110 Visentium (*Bisenzio*), central Italy. a
111 *Vix*, N.E. France. e
112 Volsinii (*Orvieto*), central Italy. a
113 *Vonitsa*, N.W. Greece. d
114 Vulci, central Italy. a

Note: This list does not include sites in the Peloponnese south of lat. 37° 30′, for which see Ill. 7. For decorated vases the list is compiled mainly from Stibbe's catalogue; for plain vases it is based on Shefton's list in *Perachora* II, 382, n.1.

Sparta itself, as one would expect, we have, in spite of the small sample, more variety, with most of the usual shapes represented. Most common is a two-handled mug (*lakaina*) specially identified with Sparta by later writers, of which Stibbe lists sixteen, only one, in Sicily, being recorded elsewhere. The wine cup comes next with 11 examples. Other shapes include two further drinking vessels, bowls, wine jugs, mixing bowls (*krateres*) and oil-flasks (*aryballoi*). Only at Samos and in Etruria is there any comparable diversity of shapes. These include, besides oil-flasks, wine jugs and mixing bowls, some shapes not yet found at Sparta in this style, the large round bowl (*dinos*) known at Sparta in Laconian II (two from Samos and one from Etruria) and the three-handled water jar (*hydria*), of which three come from Etruria and one from Samos, as well as one each from Rhodes and Pergamum. It is interesting, too, that of the ten mixing bowls of which the find-site is known, two are from Sparta, five from Samos and three from Etruria.

The pattern of distribution, with its concentrations in the south-eastern Aegean, Africa and Sicily, suggests that the carriers may have been Samians and Corinthians. Direct Spartan contact with Tarentum, and perhaps Cyrene, cannot be excluded, but it is notable that Tarentum, which imported a variety of Spartan vases in earlier periods, took only wine cups in this, drawing the other shapes mainly from Corinth. The variety of shapes at Samos, with its long and close connection with Sparta, is not surprising, but the diversity in Etruria, including the larger vessels, suggests that pottery may have come not by way of southern Italy, but up the Adriatic and across central Italy by the metal trade route – to be discussed later in connection with bronzes – especially as Etruria was an important source of metals.

The subjects of the Laconian painters were drawn almost invariably from the common archaic stock, even though the choice and treatment are often peculiar to them, so that recognition is sometimes difficult. The only purely local subject known to me is the representation of the 'hero-relief' theme of sacrifice to the underworld gods of a fragment from the shrine of Agamemnon and Cassandra exhibited in the Sparta Museum.[4] On the other hand, there is no evidence that special subjects were chosen for the export market or for particular parts of it; the two vases which have sometimes been quoted as examples, those showing King Arcesilas of Cyrene and the nymph Cyrene with her lion were found not at Cyrene but at Caere and Tarentum respectively, and must reflect the interest of the artist, not the customer.

The Arcesilas cup, now in Paris, is the most remarkable of all Laconian vases. It shows King Arcesilas of Cyrene supervising the weighing and storage of some substance, probably wool, brought to him as tribute. The king, wearing a sun hat, sits under an awning from the pole of which hangs a large balance. Two servants pack the wool into bags, which a third weighs while a fourth writes down the tally. In a lower panel two men carry the bags to the store and stow them away. The cat under the king's stool, the lizard on the wall, the monkey and birds on the cross-pole of the awning and the stork flying across behind it all add local colour and identify the scene as African, and to avoid any mistake the king and his servants are labelled by inscriptions. The effect is heightened by the extensive use of purple for hair and clothing and for the markings of the cat, lizard and birds. The cup is unusually large, 38 cm (15 in.) in diameter, so that the detail does not appear fussy or crowded as it must in a small reproduction. The scene had clearly fascinated the artist, whether he had seen it himself or heard it described by someone who had.

15 The Arcesilas cup is unique not only in Laconian but in archaic Greek art as the representation of a contemporary foreign scene. Most of the subjects are more conventional. Some reflect the interests of aristocracies everywhere in Greece, hunting and feasting, and are often copied or adapted from Corinthian models. A common subject shows a grotesque dance
27 of padded men around a wine jar. This too is a Corinthian subject, but such dances were, later authors tell us, also associated with Sparta. They were no doubt religious in origin and connected with the worship of Dionysus; similar padded dances were performed during the carnival preceding Lent on at least one Greek island until recently.[5] War, the other aristocratic interest, is notably rare except in an obviously epic context. The one exception shows not its glory but its pathos, an elegiac picture of a fallen warrior being carried from the field by his comrades.

The Olympian gods are not common subjects, though Zeus
17 appears on two vases with the Lycaean eagle and on others in conversation with Hermes or Hera. Among heroes Heracles is, as elsewhere, easily the favourite, and several of his labours are shown. Connected with Heracles, too, were the Titans Atlas and Prometheus, shown on a fine cup by the Arcesilas Painter. Sphinxes and winged horses are favourites, either as the main

15 (*opposite*) The Arcesilas cup. Ht 20 cm; diam. 38 cm

16 Atlas and Prometheus; cup by the Arcesilas Painter. Diam. 20.3 cm

17 Zeus Lycaeus and eagle; cup by the Naucratis Painter. Diam. 18 cm

18 Sphinx; cup by the Naucratis Painter. Diam. 20.5 cm

19 Youth with winged horses; cup by a follower of the Naucratis Painter

subject or as ornaments, and a feature peculiar to Laconian vases is the presence of winged spirits hovering around the main 21
figures, carrying wreaths to a victorious rider or inspiring the flute-girl at a banquet. There are some scenes from the epic poems. One shows the blinding of Polyphemus from the 20
Odyssey, but the favourite topic is the ambush of Troilus by 23
Achilles at the well, from the *Cypria*. This lent itself to the Spartan painter's love of detail, and was so popular that it was sometimes reduced to a kind of symbolic shorthand.

20 Odysseus blinding Polyphemus; cup by the Rider Painter. Diam. 21 cm

21 Youth on a horse, with attendant spirit and birds; cup by the Rider Painter. Diam. 17.8 cm

22 Revellers with mixing bowl on stand; cup by the Rider Painter. Diam. 10 cm

23 Achilles in ambush; cup by the Rider Painter. The hare, the symbol of timidity, represents Troilus. Diam. 18.5 cm

Painted vases represented at any time only a small fraction of the Laconian potters' output. Most people were content with plain red or black ware, decorated if at all with simple bands. In the first half of the sixth century a finer ware, attractively shaped and covered with a glossy black paint, sometimes with a single bold ornament in the form of a star or rosette, was exported even more widely than the figured ware, from Emporiae in Spain to Berezan and Sinope on the Black Sea, in the form of oil flasks, mixing bowls, and deep cups.

Unfortunately we know nothing of who the painters and potters were or of how the industry was organized. The small number and highly developed style of the figure painters of Laconian III and IV suggests a specialized and perhaps superior profession. They would not have been tied, as the potter was, to the wheel and kiln, and seem to have shared the interests and beliefs of the upper class. Two at least could write, and the difficulty they often found in adapting their picture to the round frame of the cup suggests that they may have been more used to a larger rectangular surface. That both painters and potters were native Laconians is proved by their roots in the local tradition. They are generally supposed to have been *perioeci* and this may well have been so, but the discovery of a kiln with the family graves of the proprietor inside one of the 'quarters' of the city, and of a claypit on its outskirts show that at least until the sixth century the craft was carried on inside the town and so probably by or on behalf of Spartans in the narrow sense. Such trades may have been pursued in their spare time by some of the poorer Spartiates or by the inferior citizens of whom we know little, younger sons or men who had for some reason lost or forfeited their lots. When Herodotus tells us that in his time 'all the Greeks, but especially the Lacedaemonians' had learnt from the Egyptians to despise hand workers, clearly the reference is to occupation, not status.[6]

24 Heracles and the centaurs; bowl (*dinos*) by the Rider Painter. Ht 26.5 cm

25 Boar hunt; cup by the Hunt Painter. Diam. 19.5 cm

26 The warrior's return; cup generally attributed to the Hunt Painter about 550, but thought by some scholars to be as late as the end of the century. The 'port-hole' effect of a round picture cut out from a rectangular original is typical of Laconian vase painters, and especially of the Hunt Painter. Diam. 15 cm

27 Padded dancers, with mixing bowl and jug; cup by the Hunt Painter. Diam. 20.5 cm

28 Ibex; cup by the Hunt Painter in his later (Lac. IV) period. Diam. 19.5 cm

29 Hunters in a wood; fragment of a bowl by a follower of the Hunt Painter. This, like the cup in Ill. 28, is in the painter's later style, in the third quarter of the sixth century

30 Boar hunt; cup by the Allard Pierson Painter. Compare this late (540–520) version with the earlier work of the Hunt Painter (Ill. 25).

4
The Terracottas

31 Head of a warrior with pointed helmet, from Amyclae. Ht 11.5 cm

At all Greek sites small figures or mould-made reliefs of baked clay are among the commonest finds, and Sparta is no exception. They occurred in large quantities at all three main sites, and in lesser numbers at minor shrines at Sparta and elsewhere in Laconia. More recently an enormous number were discovered in a dump associated with the shrine of Agamemnon and Cassandra at Amyclae. All come from dumps of discarded offerings and are in fragmentary condition, having apparently been deliberately broken to prevent re-use. They were made expressly for dedication, no doubt near the shrine at which they were offered, and were religious in subject.

The earliest terracottas at Sparta were simple hand-made figures of horses and cattle, and occasionally men, such as a child might model. These appear first about 750 and become common in the seventh century, continuing with little change well into the sixth. From the end of the eighth century onwards, however, the influence of eastern bronze work is reflected in a few works of remarkable quality.

The earliest of these are a pair of heads from Amyclae, the first of a clean shaven warrior with pointed nose and staring eyes, wearing a conical helmet of the type found on Geometric bronzes 31 from Athens and Olympia, the second, less well preserved, of a woman with ear-rings and a low cap (*polos*). She has the same large eyes as her consort, and no doubt her nose, now broken, was similar to his. They belong to the last quarter of the eighth century. Details such as eyes, hair, and the woman's ear-rings and cap were painted. The bodies, now lost, may have been cylinders shaped on a wheel. Both were meant to be seen in profile, and show already the lean angular outlines characteristic of Geometric art.

Somewhat later, and already more typically 'Laconian', is a
32 plastic vase in the shape of the head of a bearded man, with an opening at the bottom, from the temple of Orthia. In this the curves of the nose and beard subtly modify the rectilinear Geometric convention. The modelling is flat and this head too is conceived in profile, but it has a lively and humorous realism which is distinctly Spartan. It belongs to the first quarter of the seventh century.

About this time the use of a mould, long known in Syria, reached Greece, and with it a quite different approach to the representation of the human head. The new technique favoured flat modelling, with the face shown from the front rather than in profile and in the new style, known to us as Daedalic, it was made to conform to a preconceived ideal formula rather than being allowed the realism that had begun to grow out of Geometric.

32 Vase in the shape of a head, from the temple of Orthia. The opening is at the bottom, the vase being apparently meant to hang upside down. Ht 5.5 cm

33 Head of a woman; terracotta relief. Ht 10.5 cm

The transition from Subgeometric to Daedalic is well shown in the relief of a woman's head from the acropolis, which is one of 33 the earliest mould-made figures to be found in Greece. The pointed nose and chin still follow the Geometric convention, but the triangular, flatly moulded face and the straight fringe above unnaturally high-set eyes are already Daedalic. The bright colours of the paint are unusually well preserved.

In the earliest Daedalic reliefs the face is shaped as a triangle, with a straight fringe of hair low down above the eyes as the base and a pointed chin as the apex, the cheeks being defined by straight lines. In the middle style the face was lengthened and the chin rounded, and finally the face was once more shortened with the chin cut off square to form a trapeze. This style was fully developed by 750 and lasted until about 720. It prevailed in most of mainland Greece. Though also applied in other materials, such as ivory, bronze and stone, it probably began with, and is most characteristic in, mould-made terracottas, and of these the

34 Head of a youth; Early Daedalic terracotta relief from the temple of Orthia. Ht 6 cm

35 Three terracotta figures: Post-Daedalic head of a goddess wearing a *polos*; Middle Daedalic cup in the shape of a head; replica of the cult-figure of Orthia. Jenkins dates the cult-figure between 670 and 655, but its resemblance to the font-support from Olympia (Ill. 81) suggests that it may be rather later. Hts 6 cm, 6 cm, 8.7 cm

36 Head of a youth; post-Daedalic terracotta, approaching the Archaic type. Ht 15 cm

most complete series is that from Sparta. This covers the whole development of the style from its beginning until its disintegration and the return to a less abstract approach as the century ended.

At the temple of Orthia, which yielded the largest number of terracottas, the types and even many of the moulds had been established before the end of the seventh century. These types were neither numerous nor elaborate. The majority are female figures representing the goddess, alone, enthroned with a consort, with a lion, or on horseback, sometimes astride, sometimes side-saddle. There are examples of a head between two 38
horse-heads, found also in ivory and lead. A particularly well 39
executed type, found exclusively with Laconian I pottery and so belonging to the third quarter of the seventh century, is that of a naked female figure showing clearly the influence of the Syrian

38 Goddess riding side-saddle, from the temple of Orthia. This type was most common at the Menelaeum, where it may have been connected with a cult of Helen. This example belongs to the third quarter of the sixth century. Ht 10 cm

37 Naked goddess; terracotta statuette. Ht 11 cm

Astarte, which is the ancestor of the bronze nude female statuettes, whether these represent votaries of Orthia or Aphrodite, of the sixth century. A group representing the typical sixth-century naked youth is somewhat later. Small animals and grotesque figures are found at all levels. The dedication of terracottas continued here through the fifth century and into the fourth, but after 600 they are generally stereotyped and of indifferent quality.

On the acropolis the finds were in general similar, including many of the typical Daedalic reliefs of female heads, but with no apparent reference to the cult of Athena. The stratification here does not allow close dating, but most of the terracottas, and all those of interest, seem to belong to the seventh century. At the Menelaeum about half of the identifiable figures were found with Laconian II pottery, and so belong to the years on either

39 Head of a youth between horse heads; terracotta pendant, probably copied from an original in ivory, such as that shown in Ill. 63. Width 7 cm

side of 600. The types here are more varied than at the other two temples, but appear unrelated to the cult, unless the numerous equestrian figures are in some way related to Helen; most of these are later than Laconian II. Animals are numerous, and include, as well as the common domestic species, lions, a hare and a monkey. A finely worked head and neck of a horse in an unusual white clay, reminiscent in style of ivory carvings, is most probably imported. From the Geometric period come a considerable number of grotesque figures, including a man kneading bread, and a curious type of a figure with a pointed hood or mask reaching to the neck with two eye-holes, which may have been mounted.

So far, the picture presented by the main Spartan sites is of a craft reaching maturity early and, in spite of continuing demand, settling after the seventh century into a state of stereotyped mediocrity. This picture, however, must be modified in the light of more recent finds by Christou at the site of the shrine of Agamemnon and Cassandra at Amyclae. Here, in a single concentrated dump containing material from the Geometric to the Hellenistic period, a large number of terracotta relief plaques were found including a number of good quality from the sixth and fifth, and even the fourth, centuries. Most numerous are a series of plaques, some of unusual size – the largest measures 45 cm × 40 cm (18 in. × 16 in.) – which reproduce various forms of the theme of the 'hero reliefs': a seated male figure, with or without a female consort, holding out a cup with a snake rising to drink from it, or a seated man receiving an offering from a standing woman. There is also a fragment of a vase with the same scene. Terracottas of this subject had previously been known only in a few examples of crude design and probably late date from a small shrine by the Eurotas above the temple of Orthia, and one from Angelona in southern Laconia. The new finds are of much higher quality, and their number proves that they must be connected with a cult related to the shrine, doubtless that of the underworld god and his consort, with whom Agamemnon and Cassandra were identified, and not with a cult of ancestors or the family. Other subjects include a galloping horseman, a rider on a rearing horse, Heracles fighting a snake, and a youth with a crown of palm fronds. Here we have fresh evidence of an artistic tradition continuing through the fifth century and perhaps beyond.

40 Scent bottle in the shape of a monkey. Ht 6 cm

Figures of men or animals in the form of flasks for scent or oil were never common at Sparta, but some have been found dating from late Geometric to Laconian III or IV, as well as a few imported from eastern Greece. The majority were found with Laconian I or II pottery. The most usual shape is a female head or bust of Daedalic style, but they include a helmeted head, a partridge and a monkey.

During the prevalence of the Daedalic style, mould-made reliefs of female heads precisely similar to those of the votive plaques and shallow reliefs of gorgon masks were sometimes used as additional ornaments on vases of the larger kinds, either supporting the handles or on the neck, in imitation of bronze vessels such as the water-jars to be discussed later.

Much more elaborate use of relief ornament was made on the
41 large earthenware jars, around 70 to 80 cm (2 ft 6 in.) high and 60 cm (2 ft) in diameter, of which a complete and very fine specimen was found by Christou in 1960 in its original position in a group of graves associated with a potter's kiln between the acropolis and the river. A similar jar, lacking the handles, had been found in 1926 in the Roman theatre at the foot of the acropolis, where it had been re-used to store water, and some twenty more have been identified from fragments found in various parts of the town. Only with Christou's discovery, however, has it become possible to understand their form and purpose. In particular, the ornate volute-shaped handles of the new jar make clear their relation, suggested earlier by Christou, to the great bronze mixing bowls such as that of Vix.

One side of these jars is covered with panels of figures and patterns in relief, the other is plain, and they seem to have been buried, lying on the plain side, in the grave mound, not used as markers above it. The decorations must therefore be symbolic in intention, not for display. Earthenware jars of similar form with reliefs have been found in Crete, in Boeotia and in the Cyclades; the Spartan jars seem from their style to be later than the others, and perhaps influenced by the Cycladic. There is no external evidence for their date; the graves associated with the kiln

41 Large earthenware mixing bowl or *amphora* with reliefs, from a grave in Sparta. Ht 67 cm; diam. of mouth 44 cm

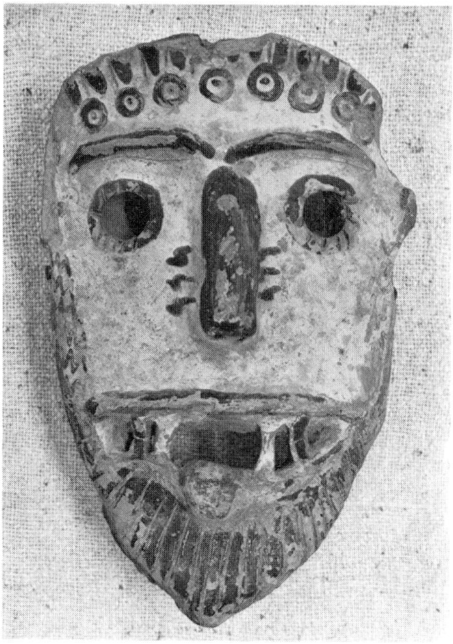

42 Old woman; terracotta mask. Ht 17.5 cm

43 Gorgon; terracotta mask. Ht 16 cm

contained no dateable objects, nor do the other contexts help. On stylistic grounds Christou gives the whole series a range from about 625, the date he assigns to the jar from the theatre, to 550 for the latest of the fragments.[1] In what he considers the earliest jars, the shoulder is decorated with a conventional funeral procession of chariots and soldiers and the neck with a pattern of tongues and grooves. In the next stage, known only from fragments, a frieze of animals or mythical beasts was substituted for the neck pattern. In the final stage, of which the new jar is an example, this was developed into a scene of hunting or fighting, reflecting perhaps the interests of the deceased in life, and the lower part of the body is decorated with rosettes. The procession of chariots and soldiers in the main position is common to all, the same moulds being sometimes used for more than one jar. The handles and the areas between the panels were richly decorated with designs copied from metalwork, as probably were the main reliefs.

These jars seem to have been the product of a single workshop, possibly of a single master craftsman, though he would have had assistants, and their use lasted little more than a generation, whether because of a change in burial custom or because their maker died without a successor. Their production must in any case have involved difficult and specialized skills, perhaps like those of the modern potters of Koroni in Messenia, who alone have the secret of making giant storage jars to-day.[2]

Peculiar to Sparta, and there to the Orthia site, are the clay masks, of which a very large number of fragments were found above the level of the sand foundation of the new temple, mostly with Laconian III and IV pottery, though in the form of Silenus masks and of miniatures they continued down to the Hellenistic period. There are several standard types; heavily wrinkled beardless faces ('old women'), realistically modelled male faces 42
('portraits'), youths, soldiers, grotesque faces, sileni and 44, 43
gorgons. It is generally supposed that they are models in clay of masks of wicker and cloth worn in ritual dances, presumably in honour of Orthia, since it is only at her temple that they are found. Some have openings for the eyes and mouth and holes for strings, others do not. The most characteristic types, the 'old women' and the grotesques, have no Greek analogies, but resemble masks found at some Phoenician sites.

Because the fragments of these masks were found packed closely in refuse dumps both of which were in use for a long time, no exact chronological conclusions are possible. They do however testify to an original streak, with a fondness for the grotesque and humorous, strongest in the sixth century but persisting well beyond it.

44 Young man; terracotta mask. Ht 22.5 cm

45 Three ivory brooch-plates. The first two represent the Mistress of Wild Things, whom the Spartans identified with Orthia; the third shows a goddess and her consort with the 'tree of life', a familiar theme in Near Eastern iconography. Hts 5 cm, 4.7 cm, 5.2 cm

46 Orthia with birds; ivory brooch-plate in the Daedalic style, with the goddess shown full-face. Ht 8 cm

5
Ivory and Bone Carving

47 Crouching sphinx; ivory statuette. Length 4.5 cm

One of the surprises of the original excavations at Sparta was the discovery on the Orthia site of more than two hundred ivory carvings, complete or fragmentary, in contexts ranging from well down in the Geometric layers to the end of Laconian II, indicating a span of about a century. At the time, the only comparable group known was the somewhat later collection from Ephesus. Since then other substantial collections of ivories have been found, notably at Perachora at the head of the Gulf of Corinth and at Samos, and these include examples older and of higher artistic quality than any from Sparta, but the latter remain the most important group in number and variety. While none of them is artistically outstanding their average level is high, and they show the existence of a school of competent craftsmen working at Sparta for at least three generations. In them the oriental influences that broke down and eventually replaced the Geometric style are most clearly displayed, and in them we see the first development of a fully pictorial style and some of the earliest illustrations of the common Greek stock of myth and legend.

The craft of carving ivory had disappeared from Greece with the Mycenaean civilization, but it had been kept alive in Syria, where by the eighth century two schools had developed, one in the north based on Anatolian and ultimately Mesopotamian models, and one in Phoenicia under Egyptian influence. Early in the seventh century the art reappears independently at several places in Greece, always apparently in close association with a well-known temple whose ceremonies provided a market. Such temples, in addition to that of Orthia at Sparta, were those of Hera at Argos and Samos, of Artemis at Perachora and of Apollo at Delphi. Since ivory had to be brought from the east and required special tools and techniques for its working, it seems likely that the craft was introduced to each of these centres, and

48 Lion with prey; ivory statuette. This is the earliest of this group, with the lion of the Hittite type. Ht 3.7 cm

probably to others yet to be discovered, by immigrant craftsmen from north Syria. These quickly adapted their familiar themes to the demands of their new customers and taught their art to local apprentices, so that it became progressively more Greek in style and subject without ever quite losing its oriental character, regularly renewed by the contacts necessary to procure the raw material. At Sparta we find elements of both the north Syrian and the Phoenician styles, the former perhaps dominant at the beginning and the other coming in later. It is, however, possible that the original introducer of the art to Sparta came from a centre in southern Cilicia or in Syria where the two schools were mixed into a local vernacular. In all cases the known ivories were religious in inspiration and apparently associated only with one particular shrine; at Sparta they have been found only at the Orthia site.

There was nothing exclusively Spartan in the subjects of the figured ivories, though the Goddess of Wild Things came to be closely associated with the cult of Orthia, and the Heracles and Paris stories had special local interest. Their style, on the other hand, was distinctive from the beginning, with a consistent development subject throughout to strong eastern influences, but unaffected by any other Greek school except perhaps that of

49 Lion with prey. This is somewhat later than the previous example. showing a more developed form of the 'Hittite' lion. Ht 3.7 cm

50 Lion with prey and human avenger. In this group the lion is of the Assyrian type. Ht 3.3 cm

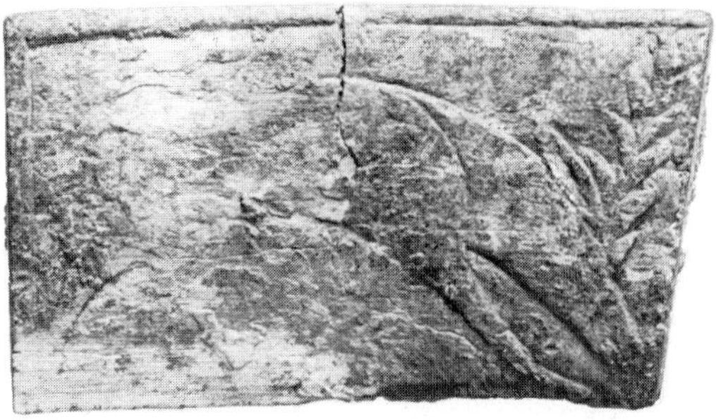

Samos. No foreign ivories have been found in Sparta; a few Spartan ivories found their way to temples in Argos, Perachora, Athens and Crete.

51 Sheep; ivory statuette. Length 5 cm

52 Grazing stag; engraved drawing on the base of an ivory statuette. Width 5.3 cm

The most numerous group, about 160 in number, consists of miniature statuettes of crouching animals on a rectangular base, the underside of which is often decorated with a design in intaglio or, less often, in relief. The oldest of these were found deep in the Geometric strata, and perhaps go back as far as the first quarter of the seventh century, and they come to an end with Laconian I, about 625. The majority represent domestic animals, especially sheep, but not including horses. The oldest of all is a very oriental sphinx, and there is an interesting group with 47
Hittite affiliations showing a lion devouring its prey. In one of 48–50
the latest of these the addition of a diminutive human figure about to plunge his sword into the lion's flank converts a static 50
group into a dramatic action picture, the beginning of Spartan narrative illustration. The designs underneath the bases are very varied and have no apparent relation to the main subject. In addition to purely abstract or decorative patterns, they include legendary beasts and winged gods, animals, birds, insects and fish. A few have human subjects: grotesque dancers, a running soldier, and a peasant setting off, mattock on shoulder, to work.[1]

The use of these objects is uncertain. Though clearly derived from the Near Eastern seals, they do not appear to have been used as seals, and many of them would have been quite unsuited to this purpose. Most of them have holes drilled just above the base, and they may have been worn as pendants during the ritual dances and then dedicated to the goddess; or they may, as the number of sheep rather suggests, have been offered as a substitute for live sacrifices, in which case the hole would have been to suspend them in the temple.

53 Crane; relief on the base of an ivory statuette. Length 4 cm

The first pictorial reliefs take the form of rectangular plates for brooches (*fibulae*) used to fasten the Dorian costume at the

54 Goat; relief on the base of an ivory statuette. Length 4 cm

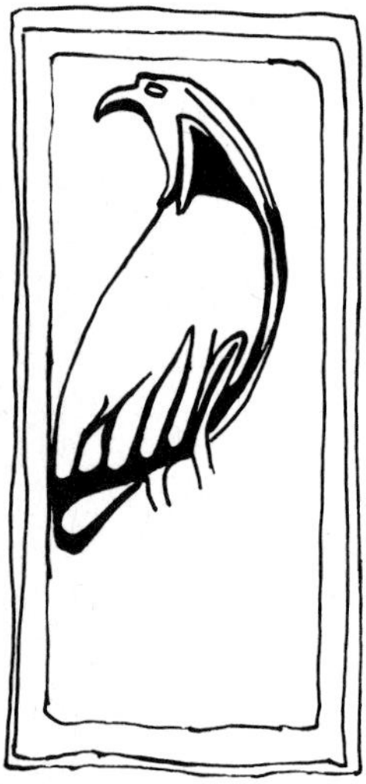

55 Eagle; relief on the base of an ivory statuette. Length 4 cm

shoulder. The oldest of these, like the oldest animal reliefs, go well back into the seventh century, and were also part of the ceremonial costume for dances such as those described half a century later by Alcman. The earliest are almost entirely Anatolian in character, but are adapted to the ritual of Orthia as a nature goddess. Two, almost identical, show the winged goddess grasping the neck of a bird in each hand. She is dressed in a long skirt with geometric patterns, and her head is turned to one side. A third, of about the same age, shows the goddess, without wings, facing a male consort across a symbolic 'tree of life'. Slightly later, she is depicted with a bulbous nose and thick lips holding a bird with one hand (the other is lost) while a snake rises in a spiral beside her. The theme of the 'Mistress of Wild Things' became a characteristic one in Spartan art, as did the snake, which perhaps symbolized a link with the powers of the underworld.

Still in the Geometric period comes a work in a more purely Spartan tradition which shows the independence quickly
57 reached by Spartan carvers. This is a fine head of a bearded man, cut out in silhouette with details in shallow relief, which recalls

56 Heraldic eagle; relief on the base of an ivory statuette. Length 4.8 cm

57 Head of a man; ivory silhouette and relief. Ht 5.2 cm

the earlier terracotta head from Amyclae and the contemporary one from the temple of Orthia.

Apart from this head, the subjects of the Geometric period are all supernatural or exotic: winged gods and goddesses, mythical monsters and lions borrowed from the art of Anatolia or Mesopotamia. They are always shown with the heads at least in
profile according to the Geometric convention, but the crude 60
Anatolian features of the first reliefs are soon replaced by a more refined style of drawing which may owe something to Phoenicia but is already distinctively Greek.

The advent of the Daedalic style about the middle of the seventh century was accompanied by a new interest in humanity, perhaps connected with a new wave of religious teaching from
Delphi. Monsters, such as sphinxes and gorgons, are still 58–60
common, as they were throughout all Greek Archaic art, but, tamed and humanized, they are no longer awe-inspiring but benevolent, grotesque or merely decorative. The goddess and
her consort are shown as a human couple seated on their throne, 61, 62
and in three dimensions. The greater flexibility given by the

58 Monster with a Gorgon's head and the body of a griffin or sphinx; ivory relief. Ht 6 cm

59 Three ivory brooch-plates, representing a lion, a winged goddess and a sphinx. These three are probably the work of the same artist. The ornament on the head of the goddess is the earliest representation of the headdress commonly found on sphinxes in Laconian III pottery, e.g. Ill. 18. Hts 4.5 cm, 6.5 cm, 5.2 cm

60 Pair of sphinxes; ivory relief ornament. Ht 2.8 cm

ability to show figures frontally made possible narrative illustrations of several figures in action on larger plates made by joining several pieces of ivory. The two earliest to survive represent a funeral, perhaps that of Hector, and are still almost purely Geometric in feeling. Later we find Heracles killing the centaur Nessus and fighting the hydra, Perseus and Medusa, and Prometheus devoured by the vulture. Three of these themes represent the victory of human heroes over monsters, while the fourth illustrates the myth of Prometheus, who defied the gods to bring fire to man and so make civilization possible. Two reliefs, both badly damaged, seem to show scenes from ordinary life, a fight (perhaps epic) and a hunt. Here too belongs the brooch-plate showing an armed soldier mounted on a shaggy little pony, very different from the long-backed thoroughbreds generally shown in chariot scenes, but with a head not unlike those on either side of a boy's head in a contemporary harness-ornament. 63

61 Divine couple, seated; ivory statuette in the Late Daedalic style. Compare the slightly later wooden figure at Samos illustrated in G. M. Richter, *Handbook of Greek Art*, 7th edn fig. 263. Ht 3.2 cm

62 Divine couple, seated; this statuette is in the Early Daedalic style. Notice the elaborately carved throne and the panther crouched beneath it. Ht 6 cm

63 Boy's head between horse heads; ivory relief, perhaps a harness ornament. Ht 4 cm

64 Soldier on horseback; ivory brooch-plate. Ht 4.1 cm

65 Pegasus; ivory comb. Length 5 cm

66 Ibex grazing; ivory comb. Length 8 cm

67 The judgment of Paris; ivory comb. Length 8 cm

68 Warship leaving port; ivory relief. The shape resembles a comb, but the relief is too large and there is no sign of teeth. It was probably attached to a piece of furniture. Length 24 cm

69 Ivory cup in the shape of a head. Ht 4.5 cm

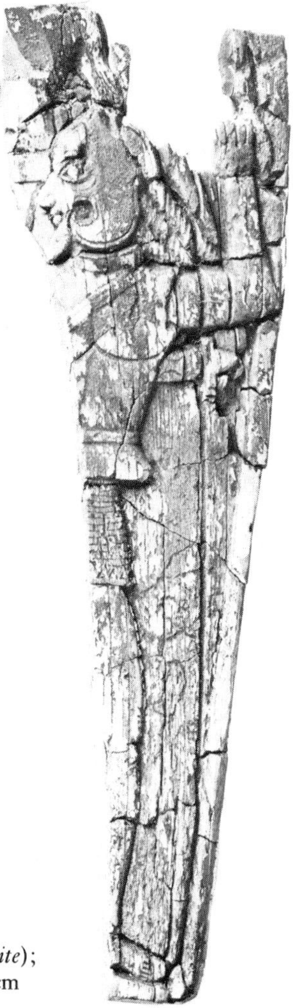

70 Foot soldier (*hoplite*); ivory relief. Ht 11.2 cm

71 Pelican; impression from a bone seal. The top of the seal has a Middle Daedalic head of 650–625. Length 3 cm

The same period saw the production of most of the semicircular ivory combs, derived from eastern models but in Greece apparently peculiar to this site, decorated on both sides with reliefs, usually in a crude but lively 'popular' style. Besides the usual range of real and mythical animals, their subjects include a number of scenes from the epic poems, showing the wide-spread popularity of these stories. Like the decorated brooches, these combs will have been part of the costume for the sacred dances, not articles of daily use.

72 Head of a soldier; bone silhouette and relief, probably part of a full-length figure. Ht 2 cm

Though the third quarter of the century was the most prolific
period of Spartan ivory carving, the craft continued until the end
of the century or a little later. Indeed, two of the largest and most
elaborate reliefs, that of a warship leaving port and that of a fully 68
armoured foot-soldier, were found immediately below the layer 70
of sand laid down for the building of the new temple about 575
BC, though they must have been carved some years earlier, and
an ivory cup in the shape of a head, of which the context is not 69
recorded, looks like fifth-century work. Early in the sixth

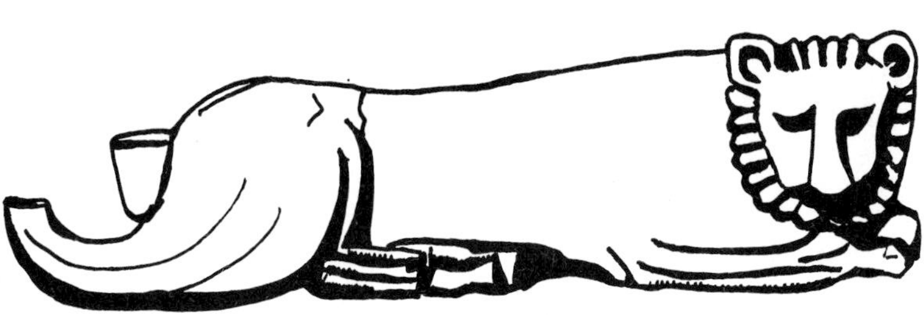

73 Lion; bone ornament. Length 8.5 cm

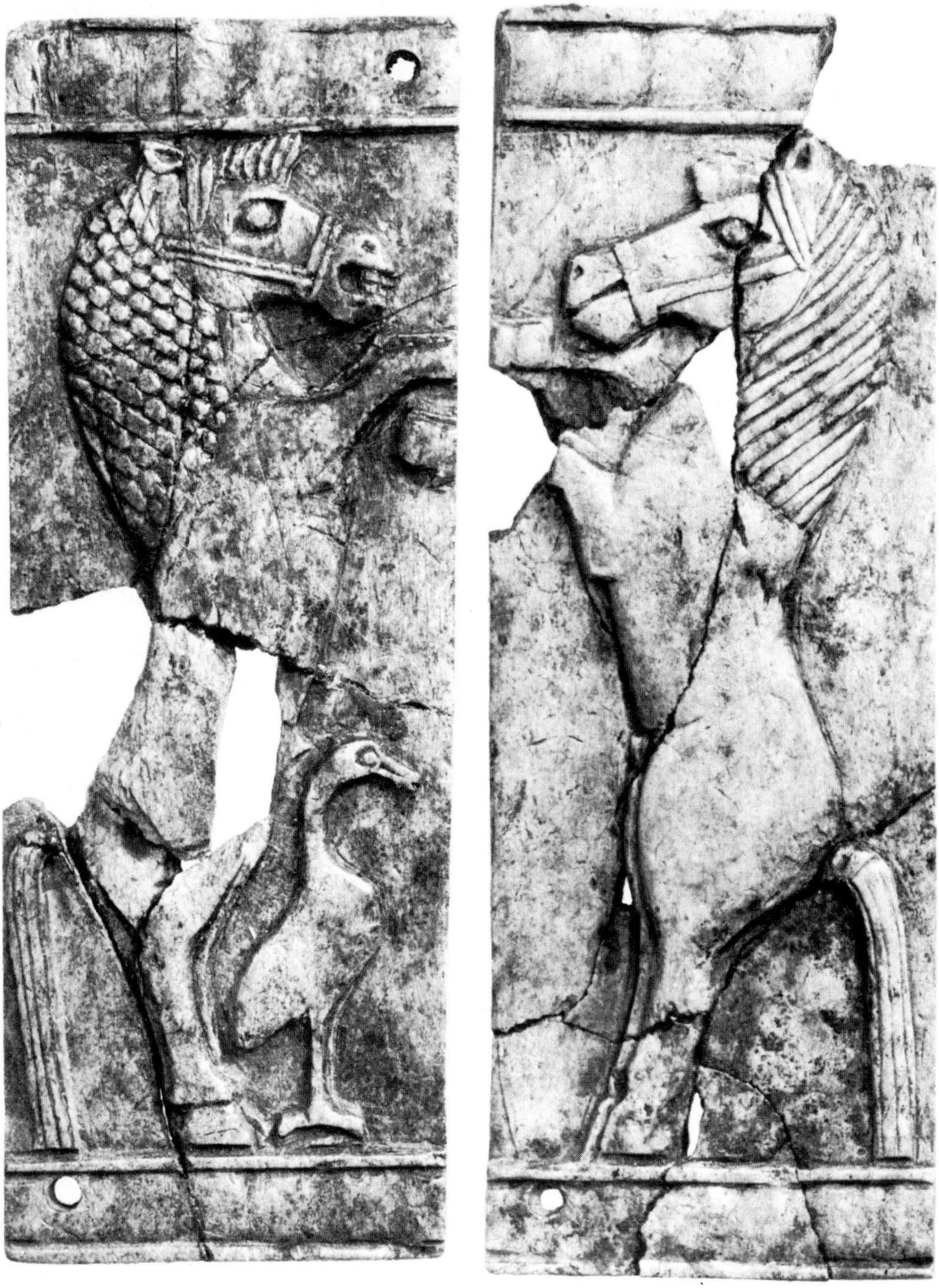

74 Pair of facing horses; bone ornaments. The slight difference in height and the different treatment of the manes make it doubtful whether these were in fact a pair. Hts 9 cm, 9.2 cm

75 Bone relief of Orthia. A number of these reliefs were found in contexts with dates from 650 to 450. They were probably copies of a cult image of about 650. Ht 12 cm

76 Bone relief of Orthia. Another version of the cult image, somewhat later in style than the type shown in Ill. 75, resembling the font-support from Olympia (Ill. 81). While the first type is Syrian in origin, this goes back to a Phoenician model like the figure from Sidon now in the British Museum (London, BM 127136; *AO* fig. 117). Ht 11 cm

century, however, the import and use of ivory came to a sudden end, as it did also elsewhere in Greece, probably as a result of the Assyrian invasions of Syria which culminated in the siege of Tyre in 573 BC. Bone had for some time been used as a cheap substitute for ivory, especially for mass-produced articles such as replicas of the cult-image of Orthia or seals topped with a Daedalic head in relief. Now that ivory was no longer available, the same techniques were used to produce ornamental bone plates for the decoration of furniture. Bone, however, could never take the place of ivory. This was done in part by bronze, while the primacy in pictorial art, and much of the repertory of the ivory-carver, passed to the vase painters of Laconian III.

77 Water bird; bone ornament for a box or furniture. Twenty-one examples of this type of ornament were found, the majority with Laconian III and IV pottery (575–525), the rest up to Laconian VI (third century). Ht 8 cm

78 Griffin; bone seal from the Orthia site, found with Geometric, Protocorinthian and Laconian I pottery, and so dated *c.* 650. Diam. 3 cm

6

Sculpture in Stone and Marble

79 Goddess; limestone relief from Mistra. Ht 4.5 cm

Of Spartan sculpture in stone relatively little remains, and hardly any in the round or of monumental scale. This is partly because the deserted site of Sparta served for centuries as a quarry for limeburners, and partly because the local marble, blue or grey in colour, was hard to work and unsuited to delicate effects, so that major Spartan artists such as those whose work at Olympia Pausanias describes preferred other materials such as bronze, or cedar plated with gold and ivory.[1] Nevertheless a local tradition with a distinctive style expressed mainly on a small scale and in relief, and largely popular in character, can be traced from the seventh century to Hellenistic and even Roman times.

The earliest surviving example comes from the beginning of Hellenic sculpture. It is a figure of a woman in the early Daedalic style of the second quarter of the seventh century, carved in relief on one side of an irregular limestone slab which may have
79 supported a lustral basin or a bowl for sacrificial offerings, and which was found built into a medieval wall at Mistra.

Next comes a series of more elaborate supports for lustral basins (*perirrhanteria*) required by the enclosed temples being built throughout the Greek world in the second half of the seventh century, which have been plausibly connected with Sparta, where some of them were certainly made. In these, the
80 basin was supported by three or four goddesses around a central column or back-to-back, wearing a flat cap (*polos*) and long gown (*peplos*) lightly belted at the waist. Each stands on a lion lying on the base, which she holds on a leash and sometimes also by the tail. The whole support, including the base, but not the basin or a separate supporting plinth, was carved from a single block of stone about a cubic yard in size.

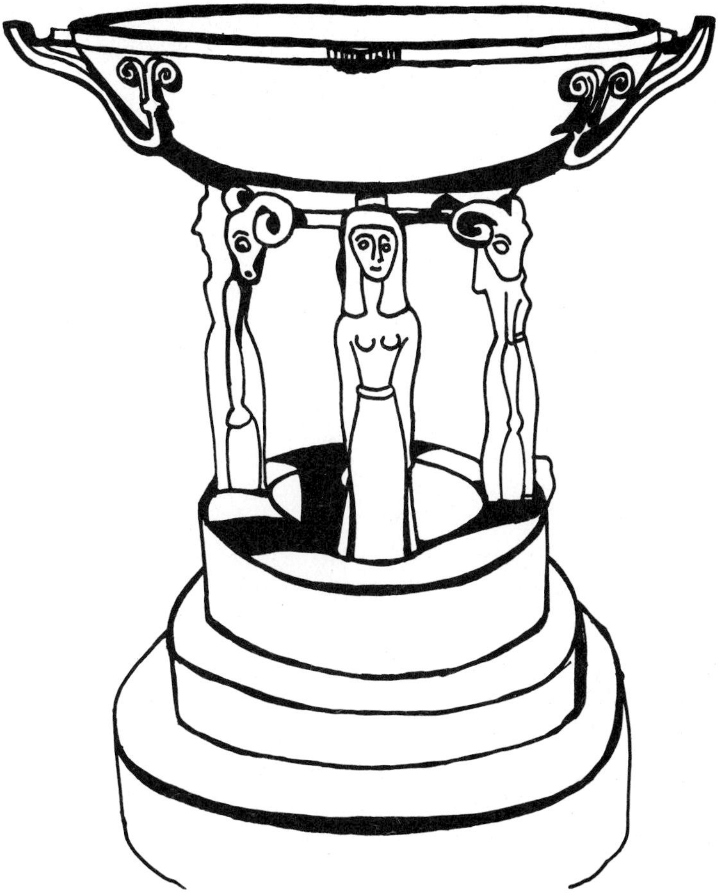

80 Font supported by three goddesses. Ht (with base) 126 cm

81 Goddess, part of a font-support from Olympia. Ht 48 cm

82 Lion from the base of a font from Sparta. Ht of lion 21 cm

Nine of these supports are known. As well as Sparta and the Amyclaeum, they come from Samos, Rhodes, Corinth (two), Boeotia, Delphi and Olympia, and range in date all through the Daedalic and into the following transitional period. At Sparta several fragments of bowls, some perhaps of later date, have also been found.

In spite of differences in the details of the design and those due to the span of time represented, the similarity between them is so strong as to make it likely that they were all the products of a single workshop. If this is so, there is a strong case for locating it at Sparta, or at least in Laconia, perhaps in the little town of Caryae near the road north to Tegea. The material is in every case but one the bluish marble characteristic of Laconian work which, though found elsewhere, does not seem to have been used for sculpture in other places; the exception is a yellowish limestone which could well be Laconian. The subject of the lion-taming nature goddess is appropriate to Sparta, and the nearest analogies in style are Spartan terracottas and ivories. The one found at Sparta, of which only the base with the lions survives,
82 and that from the Amyclaeum are certainly local, and there is no doubt on grounds both of style and material that that from the
81 temple of Hera at Olympia, on which we know from the roof tiles that Spartan craftsmen were employed, is also of Laconian workmanship. It is the latest of the series, from the last years of the century, and the post-Daedalic face, rectangular in shape instead of triangular, with its exaggeratedly square jaw and severe mouth closely resembles contemporary terracotta and bone figures of Orthia.

A Laconian artist may also have been responsible for a much more important work in the same temple, the colossal seated
83 figure of the goddess, of which only the battered head remains. This shows a further advance from the Daedalic formula in the direction of realism, with its high forehead, egg-shaped face and curved mouth anticipating the 'archaic smile', but the face is still flat and meant only to be seen from the front. This impressive figure would form part of a series of smaller seated figures of the late seventh and early sixth centuries, of which two early examples have been found in Sparta and two others, from Asea and Aghiorgitika, near Tegea, are probably also Spartan. Except the last, these are all headless and badly worn.

In spite of these rather groping post-Daedalic experiments the change to the Archaic style, with its three-dimensional approach, sculptural moulding of limbs and drapery, and return to profile in

83 Head of Hera from Olympia. Ht 48 cm

preference to frontal treatment, was as abrupt as the change about the same time from Laconian II to Laconian III in vase painting. From the next period we have scarcely anything in the round, but a number of reliefs, mostly of a popular character and often conservative and unsophisticated in style, which are extremely difficult to date except in the widest limits. In the absence of a comparative analysis and of recorded archaeological contexts even their relative chronology is uncertain.

The date of the change is fixed by a group of small carvings in very soft limestone, in incised outline, or relief, or completely cut out in silhouette and partly rounded, which were all found in or near the layer of sand laid down as the foundation for the new temple of Orthia after the old had been destroyed by a flood between 580 and 570 BC. These seem to be connected with the new building, of which the pediment with two facing lions and certain other architectural details are sometimes represented.

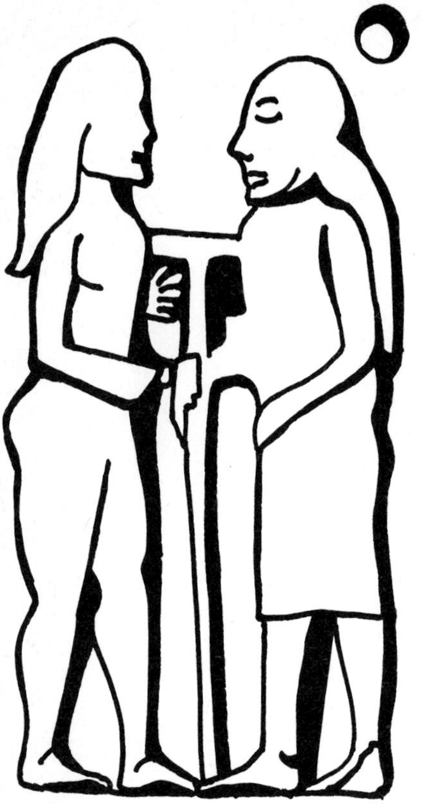

84 Man and woman facing across a T-shaped staff; shallow relief on soft limestone from the temple of Orthia. Ht 24 cm

85 Grotesque dancer; shallow relief on soft limestone. Ht 15 cm

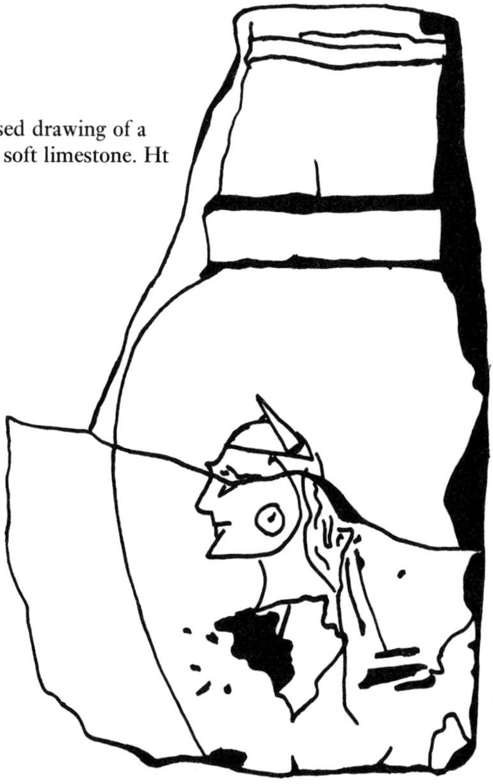

86 Incised drawing of a head on soft limestone. Ht 20.7 cm

87 Horse; shallow relief on soft limestone. Ht 9 cm

Some bear inscribed dedications to Orthia. The style is informal and mostly crude, but clearly belongs to the new school; they look like scribblings of workmen on scraps of left-over material from the building. Among them are a flat relief of a man and woman facing one another, both grasping a T-shaped staff, rather 84
like the early Dioscuri reliefs, and one, of which only the lower part remains, of two facing male figures with spears, perhaps the Dioscuri themselves. There is an energetic sketch of a grotesque dancer like those on the base of some ivory seals, while another 85
shows a warship under sail in simple incised outline. The most interesting is a sphinx, cut out and partly carved in the round, with full-face head and body in profile. The best have an 88
attractive freshness, but their main interest lies in the fact that they can be fairly precisely dated and that they provide a link between the later ivories and the reliefs.

It was in the sixth century, after 575, that many of the open-air shrines of popular deities and heroes which were still a feature of the Laconian landscape in the second century AD were adorned with reliefs generally cut on one side of an irregular or roughly

88 Sphinx; silhouette and relief in soft limestone. Ht 20 cm

89 Menelaus wooing Helen; relief on four-sided slab of blue-grey marble. Ht 67 cm

shaped stone slab fixed in the ground by a projection at the bottom. A considerable number of these, mostly from Sparta and its neighbourhood but some from outlying places such as Khrysafa to the west at the foot of the Parnon range and Yeraki in central Laconia, have survived.

The oldest of these is different in form from the rest, being a four-sided pyramid cut off at the top. The two wider sides carry episodes from the story of Helen and Menelaus; on the narrow
89 sides a snake curls upwards. In the first of the narrative scenes Menelaus embraces his young bride who offers him a wreath; in
90 the second, Helen, dressed for travelling, is threatened after the capture of Troy by Menelaus with his sword, which she is pushing aside. In both scenes Menelaus is shown as nude, though in the first he wears a headband; the figures are in profile

90 Menelaus and Helen meet at the sack of Troy; relief on the reverse side of the slab (see Ill. 89)

except that in the first scene Helen's body is half-turned to the front. The snakes indicate that the personages were worshipped as heroes, dwelling in the underworld. The style, heavy but strong, is already typically Laconian, and the date is early in the second quarter of the century.

Close to this in style, though somewhat later, are two very similar reliefs of a girl dressed in a long gown with her hair falling in a mass down her back, and holding a lotus flower. On the 91
better preserved of the two is carved the name of the person making the dedication, Anaxibios. The girl is an idealized representation of a votary, or perhaps a maiden goddess.

The first relief dedicated to Helen's brothers, the Dioscuri Castor and Pollux, also belongs to the second quarter of the century. They were the special protectors of Sparta, taking it in

91 Girl holding a flower; votive slab dedicated by Anaxibius; from the acropolis. Ht of figure 84 cm

turns, according to legend, to live in an underground mansion at Therapne while the other dwelt with the gods on Olympus. In the earliest relief the brothers face one another under the *dokana*
92 (two poles with a crossbar) which was one of their symbols; snakes rear up on the sides of the slab. A later version, altogether lighter and more graceful, comes from towards the end of the
93 century. Between the brothers are two tall jars (*amphorae*), another of their symbols, while in a pediment above two snakes support Leda's egg, from which Helen was born. Later, the brothers are shown with a variety of attributes, sometimes with Helen between them, sometimes leading or riding horses. The series lasts through the second century and into Roman times.

About the middle of the sixth century a new phase begins, apparently under East Greek influence of which the engagement of Bathycles of Magnesia on the new temple at the Amyclaeum was one aspect, but which was no doubt due to the continuing trade with Samos attested by the vases. The stark simplicity of the early reliefs is softened, the forms become rounded and the drapery more flowing.

92 The Dioscuri; relief on grey marble, 575–550. Ht 66 cm

93 The Dioscuri; relief on blue marble, 525–500. Ht 53 cm

94 'Hero relief'; underworld god and consort, seated, receiving offerings from worshippers. The other relief is Sparta Mus. 3; Steinhauer xix. Ht 87 cm

The best known and by far the most numerous series of Spartan reliefs, the 'hero reliefs', do not seem to begin until well into the second half of the century. Altogether about thirty of these are known, though many only from fragments. Most come from Sparta or its immediate vicinity, but they have also been found at Khrysafa and at Yeraki; in addition clay replicas were found among the dedications at the shrine of Cassandra at Amyclae, at Angelona in southern Laconia and at the shrine north-west of the city on the road to Megalopolis. Rather more than half may date from the later sixth and early fifth centuries, the rest being Hellenistic, but it is difficult to distinguish true Archaic examples from later copies.

In these reliefs a bearded male figure sits on an elaborately carved chair, holding out a cup of a special shape (*kantharos*). In the earlier examples a snake rears up behind the chair; later it sometimes rises in front of the figure to drink from the cup. Usually the male figure has a consort by his side, holding up the corner of her veil with her left hand and holding a pomegranate in her right. Sometimes miniature figures bring offerings, a cock and an egg and pomegranate flowers and fruit. In the Hellenistic period variations are introduced, such as a naked boy pouring wine into the cup. The meaning of these figures, which, like the Dioscuri reliefs, are found only in Laconia, has been much disputed. It used to be supposed that they were the 'heroized ancestors' of a family cult, but it is now thought that they represent the god of the underworld with his consort, whose cult must have been very popular and widely diffused, and was associated at Amyclae with that of Cassandra and Agamemnon. One fragment of particularly fine workmanship of the later sixth century bears an inscription [h]ilon, and may come from the hero-shrine of Chilon seen by Pausanias. The relief showed the usual male and female seated figures and the coiled snake below the chair.[2]

Generally thought to be the earliest of the series are the two most elaborate, of which that from Khrysafa and now in Berlin is illustrated. The god turns his face towards the spectator, and its 94
roundness, the elaborate drapery and his consort's slippers with turned-up toes all suggest the influence of East Greece. The other, from the Spartan acropolis, though smaller and less well preserved, is so similar as to suggest the same hand.

95 'Hero relief', fifth century. Ht 32 cm

96 Youth offering pomegranate to snake; votive relief. Dedicated by Theoclina to 'the Boy'. Ht 26 cm

Later the design is simplified and standardized. The god, in
95 flat relief and sometimes in profile, has a short, pointed beard; there is a return to the simplicity of earlier work. This pattern continued into the fifth century, and possibly later; the type was revived, with variations, in the third.

A number of other reliefs loosely described as 'grave reliefs', but probably also from shrines, belong to the later part of this century and the beginning of the next. From Magoula comes one dating from about 530 BC of a garlanded youth with a spear or
96 staff holding out a fruit to a snake, with an inscription 'Theoclina to the Boy'. Another, the find-site of which is unknown but which is certainly Laconian, is a few years later. Now in Brussels,
97 it represents three women, probably the Fates, holding what may be a skein of wool, a ball and a spindle, dedicated to the 'The Maidens' by Sotias.

The existence of a school, or possibly a single sculptor, of distinctive style in southern Laconia at the close of the sixth and well into the fifth century is indicated by four reliefs, two from Yeraki, one from Angelona and one from the Mainiote peninsula in the far south-west of Laconia. These show a considerable similarity, especially in the treatment of the drapery, and though definitely 'Laconian' in style are unlike anything found in Sparta

itself. Those from Yeraki represent a youth or girl dancing[3] and a seated mourning youth, dating from about 500 and about 450 98
repectively. That from Angelona shows a bearded man sacrificing at an altar,[4] and that from the Maina a girl lifting her 99
veil as in the hero reliefs and pouring wine into a cup held by a figure of which only the hand remains; these belong to the early fifth century. Another fifth-century relief from Kharuda, near 100
Areopolis, on the east side of the Messenian gulf, showing a youth with a round shield confronting a snake while his helmet lies on the ground, is un-Spartan in both style and iconography, and may be an import from Ionia.

Of sculpture in the round from the sixth century scarcely anything remains. The most interesting piece is a naked figure of

97 The three Fates; relief dedicated by Sotias. Ht 27 cm

98 Mourning youth from Yeraki. Ht 37 cm

99 Girl pouring libation; part of a 'hero relief'. Ht 37 cm

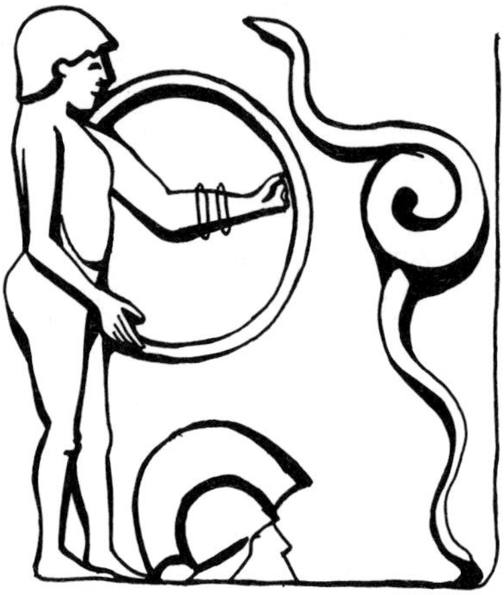

100 Grave relief from Kharuda. Ht 49 cm

101 Crested snake; fifth-century grave relief from Sparta. Ht 40 cm

Eileithyia, the goddess of birth, assisted by two attendant sprites, one of which is playing on a pair of pipes to drown her cries. This is perhaps the oldest female nude statue in Greek art, but there is nothing else resembling it and it is hard to date. The rounded contours suggest a period well down in the century, while the lack of anatomical structure and the disproportionately small arm look earlier. The better preserved of the two attendant sprites has a strong likeness to the features of a gorgon on a fragment of a basin, which Th. Karagiorga in her study of Laconian gorgons dates to about 550 BC,[5] and this may indicate the approximate date of the statue. We know that the cult of Eileithyia was associated with that of Orthia, among the ruins of whose temple two crude terracotta figurines were found, as well as various inscribed dedications to her.

102 Gorgon; relief for a gable, to avert bad luck. Diam. 32 cm

103 Birth goddess (Eileithyia). Ht 48 cm

The one undoubted masterpiece of Spartan sculpture belongs to the first quarter of the fifth century. This is the statue of a hoplite found near the Roman theatre and commonly known by
the name of Leonidas. It was not of course a portrait, but may 105
perhaps come from a memorial to the dead of Thermopylae, and certainly belongs to that period. It represents an idealized warrior, naked but for his crested helmet, calm and determined, in the act of lunging forward. The delicate reliefs on the check-pieces of his helmet contrast with the aggressive strength of the face and trunk. Unlike those we have so far considered, the statue was of imported Parian marble, but there can be no doubt of its

Spartan inspiration and workmanship. It takes its place in the tradition represented from the mid-sixth century onwards by the bronze hoplite figures, and fragments of two-sixth-century predecessors in local stone have recently been identified in the store of the Sparta Museum, a torso wearing a turned-up bell corselet and a somewhat later head with the remains of a crested Corinthian helmet.[6] Two fragmentary statues dedicated by winners in the armoured race at Olympia may be from the same hand.

With the end of the Archaic period the Laconian school of sculpture seems also to have ended, as though the Spartans were unable to make the transition from craftsmen firmly rooted in the traditions of the local workshop to the more adventurous, more individual and more cosmopolitan art of the Classical period. We have no original sculpture from Sparta of the later fifth century, and in the fourth century and later the well-to-do, like those of any other Greek or Greco-Roman provincial city, adorned their mansions with mosaics and with copies or imported specimens of the styles fashionable everywhere. Local craftsmen turned out increasingly crude versions of the popular themes, hero and Dioscuri reliefs in particular. Occasionally, however, especially in the quiet and relatively prosperous times of the Roman empire, a local artist working in the traditional local material would rise to something better, but cosmopolitan rather than
104 local in feeling, like the great boar in blue Taygetus marble that adorned the Roman theatre, or a portrait head of the second century AD from the same site.

104 Boar; statue of the Roman period. Length 88 cm

105 (*opposite*) 'Leonidas'; idealized statue of a soldier of the period of Thermopylae. Ht (without crest) 76 cm

7
The Bronzes

a

b

106 Bronze articles of the Geometric period; seated man, birds, fawn and spiral brooch. Hts (*b*) 7 cm, (*c*) 6 cm, (*d*) 4.5 cm; length (*e*) 7.5 cm; width (*a*) 4.5 cm

The bronze figures and ornaments in relief are at once the most interesting and the most controversial class of Spartan artefacts. Like the vases, many of the best were found outside Laconia; unlike the vases, there is nothing in their material or technique to distinguish them as Spartan. Since the publication of E. Langlotz's *Fruehgriechische Bildhauerschulen* in 1927 no one has disputed the existence of a Laconian school with its centre at Sparta. Its characteristics, however, have proved easier to recognize than to define, and the recognition is seldom unanimous. Thus we are forced back on a judgement of style which must always contain a subjective element. Estimates of dates, too, in spite of some help from stratigraphy, are mainly based on style, and may vary by up to half a century. Nevertheless, although certainty is unattainable and there must always remain some margin of error, the cumulative weight of probabilities is so strong as to justify the use of assumptions based on it.

The oldest bronze found at Sparta was probably imported. This little figure, curiously modern in style, of a seated man holding to his mouth an object variously interpreted as a flute, a cup, or a piece of fruit, was found in the lower strata of the Orthia site and goes back to the eighth century. A similar figure was found in the Alpheus valley, and there are examples of the same technique from Olympia and Tegea, but its home seems to be in

c

d

e

107 Ram; bronze statuette from the temple of Orthia. Ht 7 cm

108 Stag; bronze statuette from the temple of Orthia. Ht 6 cm

northern Greece and the Balkans. A little ivory figure from the Orthia site, of a monkey eating fruit, has the same pose but is perhaps a century later.[1]

The other Geometric bronzes come from higher strata, belonging to the first half of the seventh century. Apart from pins, brooches and similar toilet articles they fall into two groups. The first, which perhaps is the earlier, consists of little birds fashioned from bent wire with flattened tails and perched on rings, discs or openwork spheres. They have rings for suspension and were used as pendants. The pattern originated near the Caspian and spread through central Europe to the Alps and through northern Greece down to Tegea, whence it reached Sparta.[2] The second group consists of statuettes of domestic animals and birds such as are found on most Geometric sites, crudely modelled and on a rectangular base, often with a rough design engraved on its underside. Horses are the most common, and one type of these, characteristic of Sparta, was exported to Olympia, the Argive Heraeum and Delphi.[3] These animal bronzes continued to be produced all through the sixth century and perhaps even later.

The first bronze to exhibit a truly 'Laconian' style is a female figure from the Menelaeum, where it was found with Geometric, Protocorinthian and Laconian I pottery. This belongs to the second quarter of the century, just before the advent of the

109 Bronze shoulder pin. Length 17.25 cm

110 Ox; bronze statuette from the acropolis. Ht 3.5 cm

111 Lady from the Menelaeum; bronze statuette. Ht 13 cm

Daedalic style. Its profile recalls the terracotta head from the Orthia site, but from the front the wide forehead, large staring eyes and full lips look forward through Daedalic to the Archaic draped figures of the next century. It stands stiffly to attention, the rigidity of the pose softened by the subtle curves of the outline. It may reproduce a wooden cult-image of Helen.

111 The 'Lady of the Menelaeum' had no immediate successor. The Daedalic style did not encourage sculpture in the round, and at Sparta was practised exclusively in relief and mainly in terracotta, ivory and bone. Among suriving bronzes it is represented only by about a dozen reliefs of head and shoulders (*protomai*), whether male or female it is hard to say, from all three main Spartan sites and Amyclae. These were not cast, but

112 Mask of hammered bronze from the temple of Orthia. Ht 5.4 cm

hammered from thin sheets of bronze over a mould. This method was used for large statues such as that of Zeus seen by Pausanias at Sparta ('the oldest of all bronze statues'[4]) which may belong to this time, but these heads are small, 3.3 cm ($1\frac{1}{4}$ in.) to 9 cm ($3\frac{1}{2}$ in.) high, and were probably attached as ornaments to bronze vessels like the contemporary terracotta heads on clay vases. They represent every phase of the Daedalic style; the majority have the typical 'bead' hair-style which could be carved on the mould, but the most elaborate, illustrated here, had the hair 112
engraved on the metal after it had been shaped. Two similar but larger heads were found at Olympia, together with a mould showing that they were made on the spot, perhaps by a Spartan like those who worked about this time on the temple of Hera. There is another, of unknown provenance, at Cambridge, but the number found at Sparta and their resemblance to other heads in terracotta and ivory leaves no doubt of this being their home.

From the first quarter of the sixth century come a number of lively little ornaments in bronze, now replacing ivory for this purpose: brooches, pendants, and decorations for various kinds of furniture. Lions are the commonest motive; a favourite form has the fore-paws resting on the clasp of a brooch, with its tail, often ending in a snake's head, curved over its back in a reversed 117
S. Two examples combine the heads of a lion and a woman. Sirens make their appearance both on brooches and on other

113 Brooch with heads of a lion and a woman. Ht 5 cm

114 Sphinx; head of fibula in bronze from the temple of Orthia. Ht 7.5 cm

115 Bronze bridle-ornament from Messenia. This is a more elaborate version of the theme, originally from Luristan, found in abbreviated form in terracotta (Ill. 39), ivory (Ill. 63) and lead: see the articles by H. V. Herrmann, *JDAI* LXXXIII, 1968, and N. Yalouris, *Mus. Helv.* VII, 1950. Ht 8.5 cm

116 Brooch with two lions holding a bud. Ht 4 cm

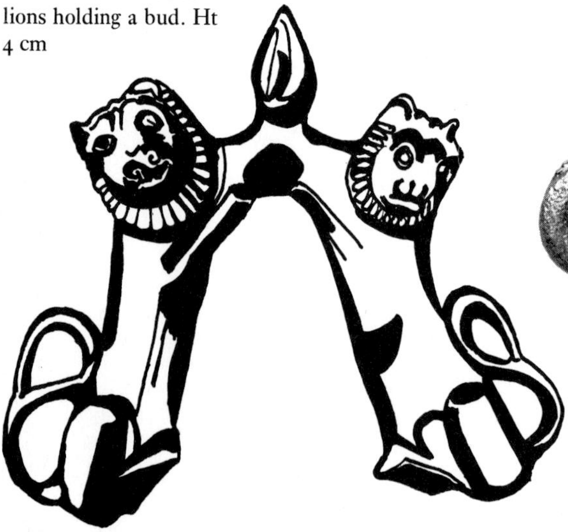

117 Brooch in the shape of a lion. Date 625–600. Ht 3.5 cm

ornaments, and pendants in the shape of a bull's head are common. Handles are fashioned with horse-heads or snakes at either end. The harness ornament with a naked youth between two winged horse-heads belongs to this time; though found in Messenia it was certainly made in Sparta, where variations of the theme in ivory, terracotta and lead are found. The little ox, flattened on one side, comes from the neck of a large mixing bowl, and the two old men facing one another above the handles of another bowl were meant to be gossiping; they show the streak of humorous realism which runs like a thread through all periods of Spartan art. Most of these were found with Laconian II pottery, and their vogue was short. By the time the temple of Orthia was being rebuilt they had gone out of fashion, along with the large and elaborate brooches and pins.

118 Ox; bronze ornament from the neck of a large bowl like that from Trebenište, now at Sofia. Found with Laconian I and II pottery. Ht 6.2 cm

119 Sphinx; bronze ornament for a box or a piece of furniture. Ht 14.4 cm

120 The gossips; bronze ornaments from the rim of a bowl. Ht 6.5 cm

121 Goddess, from the temple of Orthia, 600–575. Ht 7.7 cm

122 Goddess with fruit; bronze statuette from the acropolis. Ht 13.5 cm

The development of the Laconian figure style in the first half of the sixth century is seen in a series of draped female figures, goddesses or worshippers, from the temples of Orthia and Athena of the Brazen House, of which we illustrate the earliest and latest.

The first is still very close to the Daedalic style. The head is
121 large, and the arms are shown in low relief against the sides. The figure tapers from the shoulders to a point below the knees, where the gown widens slightly. The general effect is vaguely oriental and in some ways more primitive than the figure from the Menelaeum of fifty years earlier, but the large almond-shaped eyes, prominent nose and full curved lips are typically Laconian.

In the next figure,[5] from the temple of Athena, the size of the head is more natural, the forehead higher and the features less exaggerated. The arms are bent at the elbow, the right holding a
122 fruit against the breast. The left, broken off, perhaps held a

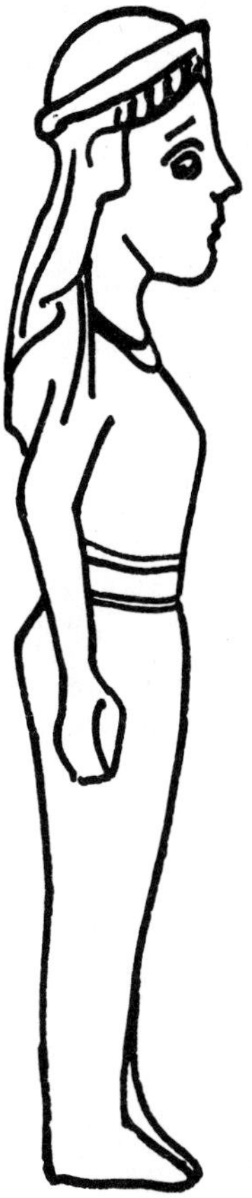

123 Woman in *peplos*, from the temple of Orthia. Ht 6.7 cm

124 Female votary with cymbals, from the temple of Orthia. Ht 11.2 cm

flower. The gown is pulled tight at the waist, curving out over the hips, from which it falls almost in a straight line to the ankles.

Another figure from the Orthia site is slightly later. The features are refined and the hair, confined by a woollen band, is drawn to a point above the forehead. The swelling of the breasts 123
is shown under the gown, which is belted and narrows from the hips to the ankles. As in the Menelaeum figure, the front and back of the dress are flat, so that the figure is almost square in section.

The cymbal player comes at the end of the series. The features 124
are natural, the elbows held out from the sides as the votary clashes her cymbals. There is a grace and naturalness about the pose far removed from the stiffness of the first figure. This figure was found with Laconian III pottery.

All these figures are clad in the Dorian gown (*peplos*), ankle-length and belted, with pleats indicated by grooves in the back of the skirt. All wear their hair in the same way, falling down the

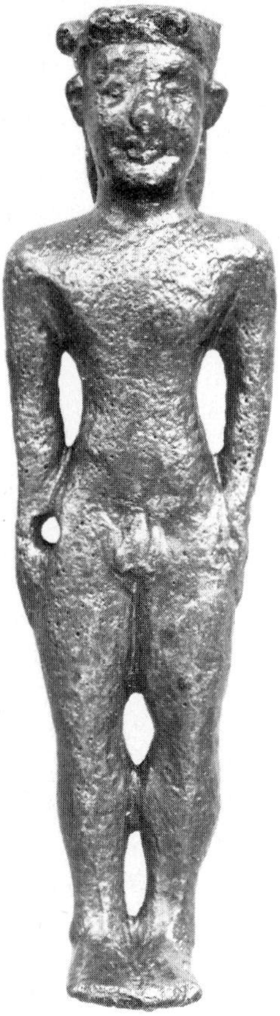

125 Naked youth; bronze statuette from the acropolis. Ht 7 cm

back in a heavy mass to the waist or below, sometimes tied with a ribbon, sometimes cut off square or to a point. The figure on the lid of the Vix bowl belongs to the same line, though in this case the hair is covered by a cloak.

The male counterpart of the Archaic draped female figure, the naked youth (*kouros*), standing to attention or with one foot slightly advanced, though less popular at Sparta, followed the same development; an example from the acropolis is very close to our third female figure in face and hair-style.[6] Also before the middle of the century were introduced several other types which were more fully developed in its second half, and can best be left until we reach this stage.

Three statuettes from the middle years of the century are so unlike other bronzes of the period that they must be the work of a single artist of unusual originality. He seems to have been especially interested in showing the male figure in movement. The first, from southern Laconia, shows an intelligent-looking, thickset man, naked, carrying a large bronze water-jar. He may be a water-carrier, but Sir John Beazley[7] has suggested that he is more likely one of the craftsmen responsible for making these jars, which, as we shall see, were a Laconian speciality. In either case, it is a study from life of a kind quite unusual among Archaic bronzes, though less so among vase paintings. The second statuette, from Olympia, represents a shrewd-faced old man walking with a stick. His hair falls in a mass down his back, his beard is neatly trimmed and his upper lip shaved in the Spartan fashion. He wears a long tunic and a cloak over his shoulders like a plaid. His discoverer guessed that he might be an umpire at the games; Beazley saw in him a master bronzesmith.[8]

The third figure shows a younger man, also bearded and with shaven lip, in a short tunic and cloak like that of the previous
128 figure, striding forward with a spear under his arm. Though generally described as a 'warrior', the lack of all armour makes it more likely that he is setting out on a hunt.

These three figures, with their closely observed realism, are purely Laconian, but they had no followers. Instead, a strong influence from Ionia is felt about the middle of the century, neatly illustrated by two stands in the form of women, purely Spartan in face and figure, but wearing not the plain Dorian gown, but the new Ionian costume with its elaborate folds. The
129 one here illustrated, a support for an incense burner, is said to come from Sparta; the other, a mirror handle, was found at Leonidhi on the Aegean coast of Cynuria.[9] Under this influence

126 Man carrying water-jar, from Feniki. Ht 8.5 cm

127 Old man with staff, from Olympia. Ht 13.9 cm

128 Hunter, from Olympia. Ht 14.3 cm

129 Stand for incense burner. Ht 21.6 cm

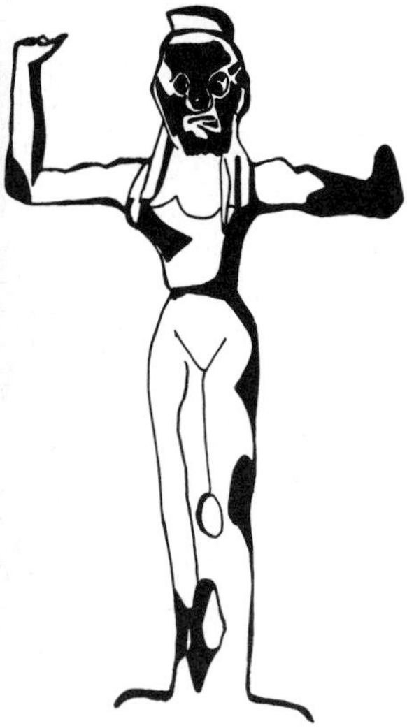

130 Bronze stand from Arcadia. The figure probably supported a basin. The head shows no trace of the attachment of a mirror. Ht 11.5 cm

the range of Laconian bronzes was widened and their style became softer and more flexible without losing its distinctive character. The second half of the sixth century was the golden age of the Laconian bronzesmith for both quantity and quality, and Spartan bronzes found their way abroad in considerable numbers. Rather than attempt to discuss the whole of this output, we shall look more closely at a few of the most interesting and characteristic types.

The first is closely related to the female figures we have already considered, but with an important difference – the figures are unclothed. Four are separate votive statuettes, but the majority were stands for polished bronze mirrors.[10]

Since Praschniker first drew attention to these in 1912 their Spartan origin has been generally accepted. Outside this group, female nudity is unknown in Archaic Greek art except, very rarely, in vase paintings of banquet scenes. This alone would raise a strong presumption of a single place of origin, which is supported by the similarity of style, allowing for the work of different artists over a long period. If we accept this, Sparta is easily the strongest candidate. Not only were the Spartans – alone of Greeks of the historical period – notoriously supposed to be tolerant of female nudity, especially among young girls, but all four statuettes, with the closely related terracotta figurines which provide a link with Phoenicia, come from Sparta, while three of the mirror-stands come from its immediate neighbourhood. No other site has yielded more than one. Of those of which the provenance is known, one is from Arcadia and three are from different places in the Argolid. Outside the Peloponnese, one comes from the acropolis at Athens and one from Vonitza in north-western Greece; further afield, there is one from Cyprus and one from Sicily. Two found respectively in Yugoslavia and the Ukraine, like one of those from Sparta, are inferior fifth-century imitations, perhaps made locally. This distribution does not suggest multiple origins, and is quite consistent with Spartan manufacture. It does suggest that the mirrors were much sought-after, whether as works of art or as curiosities.

In time, the stands span nearly a century, but their greatest period was between 550 and 525. The oldest – if in fact it is a mirror stand, which seems doubtful – is a primitive and badly preserved figure from Arcadia which somewhat resembles the font-bearer from Olympia and must belong to the early part of the century. Two, or perhaps three, look as if they belong to the

second quarter of the century, but most fall into the decades after 550, showing in their modelling the softness and delicacy that reflect Ionian influence. Of the statuettes one, the flute-player from the temple of Orthia, is earlier than 550, the other three are later. In most the hair hangs in a mass down the back as in the earlier draped statues, sometimes with one or two crossed ribbons to keep it in place, and sometimes with a short tress in front of the ear. In two of the statuettes and a few of the mirror-stands it is cut short, in the fashion of the last quarter of the century.

The meaning of the figures is uncertain. They have been associated with Alcman's chorus of maidens, with the suggestion that they symbolize the participants in the ritual dance, by whom they were dedicated, but the fact that no mirrors and only one statuette were found at the Orthia site seems to rule this out. On the other hand, there are religious implications. Most of the figures wear a neckband with an amulet, and many also a crossband with charms over the right shoulder. Several carry
cymbals or clappers; one is playing a flute and another may be 133
conducting a choir. Others hold up a flower in the gesture 131, 132
familiar on stone reliefs, and a few hold a pomegranate. The mirrors were generally supported by figures perched on the girl's shoulder; most of these are now lost, but among those preserved are several pairs of griffins and one of sirens. Sometimes the base was formed by a lion or a frog. Some of this symbolism suggests Venus, but in a rather vague way; it is such as would be

131 Naked girl, perhaps conducting a choir or dance. Ht 8.7 cm

132 Bronze mirror supported by a naked girl with flower and fruit. The attachments on the shoulder are the remains of supplementary supports like the griffins in Ill. 133. Ht (with mirror) 23.7 cm; diam. of mirror 12.2 cm

133 Bronze mirror supported by a naked girl with necklace and charm belt, with griffins. Ht (with mirror) 33.8 cm

appropriate on the toilet implement of a young girl, which she might perhaps dedicate on marriage, and the distribution suggests a secular rather than religious use. At Syracuse the mirror was found in a grave; others come from various shrines, but not so as to suggest any particular cult. The use of such mirrors with a draped support, perhaps made in Corinth, was common elsewhere in Greece, as may be seen in toilet scenes in vase paintings. If the Spartan mirrors were made in the first place for the use of the adolescent girls of the Spartan upper classes and reflect their aspirations, we have in them a new and charming glimpse of life in 'swinging Sparta'.

The more familiar side of Spartan life, 'barrack Sparta', is reflected in the next group, which consists of votive statuettes of soldiers in full hoplite armour in various attitudes of attack or march. War was an interest of all archaic aristocracies, and Sparta had no monopoly of representations of soldiers, but these are distinctive in style and their Spartan origin is confirmed by sites on which they are found. Two have the donor's name engraved on them, but they should not be thought of as individual portraits, any more than the mirror-stands. They represent types, showing how the donor wished to be seen, not how he really looked, and they are no less interesting to the social historian for that.

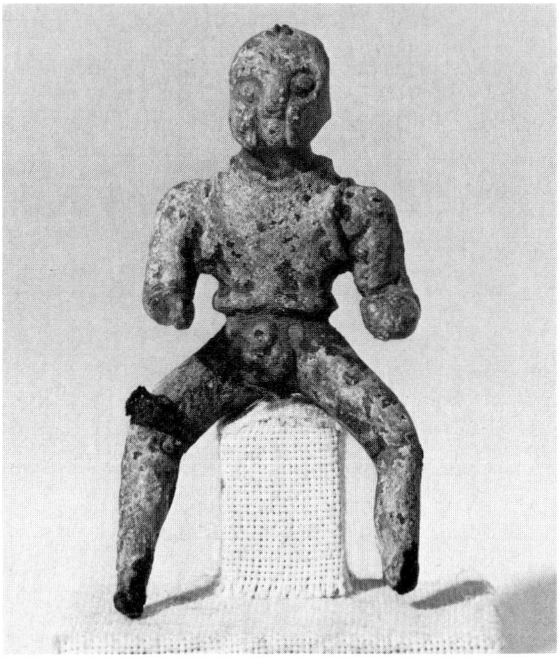

134 Mounted soldier, probably from central Italy. Bought in Paris in 1859, he had lost his original mount and arrived at the British Museum on a Roman horse picked up during his travels. I owe the suggestion that he might be Spartan to Mr Denys Haynes; he is a later cousin of the little horseman of Ill. 64. Ht 7 cm

135 (*opposite*) Soldier in battle. Bought in London, he is said to have come from Sparta. Ht 10 cm

136 Soldier in parade dress, from Messenia. Ht 15 cm

137 Soldier, probably from Dodona. Ht 10.2 cm

Curiously, none is certainly attested as coming from Sparta itself, though two are said to have done so. One is from the shrine of Apollo Maleatas high on Mt Parnon on the road to Cynuria, one from Longa in Messenia and a third from Lycosura in Arcadia. Several are from Olympia and Dodona, shrines much favoured by Spartans. One was found in each of Samos, Thessaly and north Italy; one, after what wanderings we can only guess, in southern Arabia.

In date, the statuettes extend from shortly before the middle of the sixth century to the first quarter of the fifth. The earliest is
135 that in the British Museum. Thickset and aggressive, there is nothing heroic or aristocratic about him; he is the incarnation of Tyrtaeus' good soldier, who will stand firm and hold the line with his comrades. Very different is the figure from Longa, about a quarter of a century later. Here we have, exceptionally, an
136 example of the 'officer type'. Tall and slender, with intelligent face and unwavering stare, his face reminds us of the reliefs of the big terracotta jars and the bowl from Vix. He wears his parade uniform with an embroidered tunic under his elaborately

engraved cuirass. In between, there are three main types. The first, represented by the offering of Karilos to Apollo on Mt Parnon is, like the British Museum figure, short, thickset and dogged, though as he is on the march rather than attacking he is somewhat less ferocious.[11] Another type, found at Lycosura,[12] Olympia and Samos, has a humorous, bulbous-nosed peasant face, in two cases under an exceptionally high forward-curving crest. The figure from Arabia and those at Oxford and Zurich form yet another group, small, sinewy men with fine-featured, shrewd faces, close-fitting helmets and ornamented cuirasses. All three of these types emphatically represent the common soldier, and their realism is typically Laconian. At the end of the series, a worthy contemporary of the marble 'Leonidas', comes the splendid figure found at Dodona in 1930. Tall, long-legged and muscular, his carefully dressed hair in four tresses down the back and two on each side in front, an embroidered tunic under his bell-cuirass, he combines in one figure the elegance and self-confidence of the figure from Longa with the grim determination of the fighting soldier. He is the type of the fifth-century Spartan as we meet him in Herodotus. 138

138 Soldier, from Dodona. He carried a spear in his right hand and a shield, of which the arm-grip remains, on his left arm. Ht 13.5 cm

139 Naked youth with wreath of palm leaves, carrying a cock. This statuette is in a rustic style akin to Arcadian, but the wreath shows it to be Spartan.

140 (*opposite*) Apollo, from Kosmas. Ht (with base) 18.2 cm

All of these soldiers are depicted as men of mature age, bearded and with the upper lip shaven. The younger men are represented by a group of figures of naked youths of the conventional *kouros* type but wearing a spiky wreath or crown. Two come from the temple of Apollo at Amyclae, and one each from Sparta, Olympia and Mt Lycaeum. The wreath is represented in various ways, but it seems likely that we have here dedications by participants in the dances to Apollo instituted to commemorate the victory over Argos at Thyrea in 546, at which, as Athenaeus, quoting the third-century Spartan antiquary Sosibius, tells us, the chorus wore crowns of palm leaves.[13]

These statues are all popular and even provincial in style. Of much superior quality and in line with contemporary work from other parts of Greece are two figures representing Apollo himself, wearing a thick woollen headband. The first, from Olympia,[14] belongs to the middle of the century, and shows the god with a large head, high and narrow waist and broad hips. His hair is long, with one tress over each shoulder. The left leg is slightly advanced, and each hand held some object now lost,
140 perhaps a bow and quiver. The second, from Kosmas in the Parnon range east of Yeraki, is of the first quarter of the fifth century. The left leg is advanced, and the figure is balanced on the balls of both feet in the act of taking a step. The right hand is

raised in a gesture of benediction, while the left held a bow. Though the figure is still unmistakably Laconian, none of the Archaic stiffness remains.

Finally we come to a class of large bronze vessels, three-handled water-jars and mixing bowls, of which the place of manufacture is still controversial, though as evidence accumulates it points increasingly to Sparta. Certainly their strongest affinities are to be found in Laconian art. The bodies, formed from a thin sheet of hammered bronze, have in many cases perished, leaving only the more solid cast attachments such as handles and decorations. Many of these have now been identified, though many more probably remain to be recognized. Enough complete or nearly complete examples, however, have been preserved to enable us to reconstruct the appearance of the main types.

The earliest is a water-jar of which the upper part was found at
141 Grächwil near Berne. The place of the vertical handle is taken by an elaborate group joined at top and bottom to the lip and shoulder of the jar. In the centre the winged goddess Orthia stands holding a hare in each hand and flanked by lions with curved tails. An eagle perches on her cap, on either side of which a pair of lions, back to back, stand on the rim of the vase, their feet resting on snakes which serve to join the handle to the lip. The feet of the goddess rest on a large palmette, from which a frieze of tongue-patterns runs round the shoulder of the vase. Her figure resembles those of the earlier font-supports, and suggests a date towards the end of the seventh century.

Two similar jars are known, one from its neck and shoulder, the other only from the group which formed its handle. Both were found in graves near Pesaro on the Italian coast of the Adriatic.[15] The handle of the first has as its central figure a soldier in full armour flanked by horses which stand on snakes joining the group to the shoulder. His helmet has a crest in the shape of two horse-heads, with lions and snakes on the rim on either side. The horizontal handles were joined to the shoulder by pairs of horse-heads. The other group shows two soldiers fighting over the body of a fallen comrade. One bears a large shield of the obsolete 'Boeotian' shape which shows the scene is from an epic; it has a device of two facing sphinxes. The group is very like the relief on one of the big earthenware jars from Sparta.

Though all the components of these designs are certainly of Spartan origin, the Grächwil jar, because of its somewhat

141 Neck ornament and handle of the Grächwil water-jar. Ht of jar 53.5 cm; of neck 18 cm

142 Head of a woman supporting the vertical handle of a water-jar. Ht 18 cm

barbaric profusion of detail, has been usually thought to be Tarentine work under Spartan influence. But there is no evidence that the workshops of Tarentum, or any other Greek colony in Italy, were capable so early of producing work on this scale, even if the location of the finds was consistent with such an origin. It is much more likely that the Grächwil and Pesaro jars represent an experiment by Spartan bronzesmiths, influenced by the ivory-carvers and by the makers of the terracotta reliefs for the big clay jars, but soon abandoned because of technical difficulties.

The early sixth century saw the introduction of a much simpler style, in which the attached ornament, in relief, was confined to the top and bottom of the vertical handle and the ends of the horizontal handles. In the form which became most usual, the
142 decoration consisted of a woman's head in relief at the base of the handle and sometimes a pair of lions at the top. This group takes its name from a handle in Mainz on which is engraved in Laconian characters the name 'Telestas'. Pausanias saw a work

143 Handle and part of frieze of the Vix bowl. Found in the grave of a Celtic princess dating from the last years of the sixth century; the bowl must be a generation or more earlier. Ht of bowl 164 cm; diam. 170 cm; ht of frieze 14 cm

of a Laconian sculptor named Telestas at Olympia, perhaps of this period;[16] if this is the same Telestas, the handle is one of the very few works signed by a Laconian artist. This style held the field in what was clearly a very conservative market for some thirty years.

About the middle of the century, perhaps in response to the first wave of outside competition, the ornament became more elaborate. A favourite form now had the whole vertical handle in the shape of a naked youth bending backward with his arms raised to the lip of the vessel, where they support a pair of lions. At his feet are usually a pair of sheep. This design was perhaps copied from Corinthian wine-jugs, a shape seemingly not made by Laconian smiths, but the youths can be distinguished by their Laconian features. A wider distribution inside Greece and a greater diversity of styles shows the growth of competition, especially from Corinth, and in the last quarter of the century jars from Corinth, the north-western Peloponnese and, later, Italy had driven the Laconian product from the field.

Perhaps it was the beginning of this competition that, from about the middle of the century, stimulated the production of the large and richly adorned mixing bowls (*krateres*) with volute handles, which continue side by side with the water-jars until 143, 144 about 520. The finest and best known of these is that from Vix, 145 near Châtillon in northern Burgundy; two other complete examples were found in graves at Trebenište near Lake Ochrid in Yugoslavia. Half a dozen more are known from handles only, and of others only parts of the appliqué decoration from the neck remain.

These vessels had large volute-shaped handles resting on the bust of a gorgon with snakes and lions, while the neck had a procession of figures cast separately and riveted or soldered into place. On the Vix bowl the frieze consists of alternate foot-143, 144 soldiers and chariots in the finest Archaic style 14 cm ($5\frac{1}{2}$ in.) high. The bowl itself stands 1.64 m ($65\frac{1}{2}$ in.) high and its greatest diameter is 1.70 m (68 in.). Its capacity is more than 1200 litres, and it weighs over 200 kg. The lid is preserved and on it stands a cloaked female figure 19 cm ($7\frac{1}{2}$ in.) high. With its imposing size, massive handles and formal yet lively frieze, no two of the figures quite alike, the Vix bowl is one of the most impressive works of the Archaic, or perhaps any other, period. The Trebenište bowls are considerably smaller, but still much too big for ordinary use. 145 On one the frieze is of riders at full gallop, on the other of cows. Other bowls, known only from handles or fragments of ornaments, seem to have equalled the Vix bowl in size.

Making use of fragments as well as whole vases, it is possible to trace the distribution of these vessels in some detail.[17] With some exceptions, mainly at Olympia, they have been found beyond the boundaries of the Greek world, in a pattern which differs completely from that of the painted Laconian pottery. The earliest route seems to have followed the east coast of the Adriatic to some point north of Corcyra, perhaps the colony of Epidamnus (founded in 627). Hence they crossed to Picenum, and from there overland to the head of the Adriatic and across into the Danubian plain, from which they spread west to the Alps and east to the Carpathians. Somewhere about 560 this route fell out of use, probably because of fighting in Italy. After this date the vessels, now including mixing bowls, were carried up through central Greece to Albania and then by the river valleys over the Pindus range to reach the Danube plain at its eastern end. The chance find of an early water-jar at Artand in Hungary, near the border of Romania, shows them reaching the

144 Detail of frieze on the neck of the Vix bowl.

edge of the metal-rich Carpathians, from which copper and tin had come to Greece along the even older amber route since prehistoric times.[18]

This pattern suggests that the vessels, the size of which excludes any domestic purpose, were made especially for presentation to the barbarian chiefs who controlled the essential metal routes. Even those whose find-sites lie outside the pattern will usually have had a similar purpose; for example the fortified settlement of Mt Lassois, where the Vix bowl was found buried in the grave of a Celtic princess, lay at a strategic point on the tin route from Britain to Marseilles. Some would naturally find other uses, as votive offerings or otherwise; we may recall the splendid bronze mixing bowl described by Herodotus which was commissioned by the Spartan government as a present for King Croesus of Lydia who had, incidentally, supplied them with gold for a statue of Apollo.[19]

For this trade the number required at any one time would be small and considerable skill would be called for, so that it is unlikely that more than one centre, perhaps even more than one workshop, was involved. The pattern of distribution effectively excludes southern Italy, where only a very few late examples have been found, and points strongly to the Peloponnese as the source. Here the choice lies between Sparta and Corinth. Comparatively few Corinthian bronzes of the sixth century are known, and their style is unlike that of the large vessels prior to the last quarter of the century. On the other hand these have very close analogies, both in style and in shape, with Laconian work. The mixing bowls, for example, are clearly derived from the equally large, lavishly decorated earthenware bowls with volute handles which had been used a generation earlier as grave-markers. The early water-jars from Grächwil and Pesaro are Laconian in iconography and style, and the battle scene from one of these also links them with the earthenware jars. Both the women's heads and the lions of the later water-jars have close parallels in contemporary Spartan art, and the youths of the later handles are Laconian in style and two were found in Laconia, one at Sparta and one at Monemvasia. The three-handled water-jar, common to all Greek fabrics, has a history at Sparta going back to Geometric times, and the shape of the large bronze jars is the same as that of surviving Laconian 111 examples in clay. The volute-handled form of the mixing bowl is perhaps a Spartan invention, and it too is at home in Laconian pottery. The big grave-markers are exactly analogous to the bronze bowls. Finally, the two examples which have inscriptions, the Telestas vase at the beginning of the century and the Vix bowl from its middle period, where the backs of the reliefs and the neck have corresponding letters to ensure the correct placing of the figures, both have the Laconian form of alphabet.

These vessels were naturally accompanied by tripods, several of which were preserved in the graves at Trebenište. One of these, probably intended as an ornament in its own right, is composed of three groups each of three rods, each rising fan-shaped from a lion's-paw foot to support a ring on which are alternate figures of horse-heads and reclining banqueters. A lower ring carries three lions. In the light of this, another tripod of similar construction and style from Metapontum in southern Italy, generally ascribed to Tarentum, is probably also Laconian. It has three rings, bearing respectively alternate lions and horse-heads, cows and more lions.[20]

Tripods of various kinds were among the most esteemed votive offerings at all Greek temples, but even more than the bronze vases their frames were perishable and usually only a few of the ornaments survive. This is probably the origin of many of the small figures found at Sparta, Olympia and elsewhere. The

145 Bronze mixing bowl with tripod, from Trebenište. A galloping horseman like those on the neck was found at Dodona, now in Athens, and another in Cilicia, now in the Louvre. Ht 72 cm, of frieze 8.5 cm; diam. of mouth 31.5 cm

146 Soldier putting on armour; bronze ornament from the neck of a large mixing bowl, from Edessa. Ht 12.3 cm

fine banqueter in the British Museum may be such a figure. Several similar banqueters are known of which this is the latest, probably from the last quarter of the century. The style is recognizably Laconian. Also Laconian in style and probably from a tripod is the 'running girl', now in the British Museum, a dancer rather than a runner. She was found at Prizren in what was then Albania but is now south-eastern Yugoslavia, and is to be associated with the overland metal route, not with Dodona. She may be compared with a dancing Maenad from near-by Tetova now in the museum at Skopelje.[21] A third probable tripod figure is the running Silenus from the Amyclaeum.

Thus through the whole of the sixth century and into the early years of the fifth, Sparta was a major producer of artistic bronzework. In the Vix bowl her craftsmen produced one of the masterpieces of Greek art; with the Apollo from Kosmas and the soldier from Dodona as well as the marble 'Leonidas', they come to the very threshold of the new Classical style of the high fifth century. Yet they failed to cross this threshold. Bronzes were still produced at Sparta, but they were uninspired and tasteless adaptations of Attic or other models. The original character of Laconian art and the local tradition that fostered it both vanished with the Persian wars. The few much later bronzes of quality found at Sparta were imported from one of the Hellenistic centres, Athens or Alexandria. The bronzesmith of Laconia, like

147 Banqueter; ornament from a tripod. Length 10 cm

148 Girl dancing; ornament from a tripod. Ht 11 cm

149 Running Silenus; ornament from a tripod. Ht 9.5 cm

the sculptor in stone, failed to make the transition from the craftsman's workshop, rooted in local tradition, to the studio of the new cosmopolitan artist, at home wherever his commissions took him and working in a common Hellenic idiom. Even at the beginning of the fifth century Athens was drawing to herself artists from all over Greece, and at least one Laconian, Gorgias by name, worked on the acropolis before 480.[22] The polarization that followed the Persian wars, and the cosmopolitanism of the new fashion spelled the end of Laconian art.

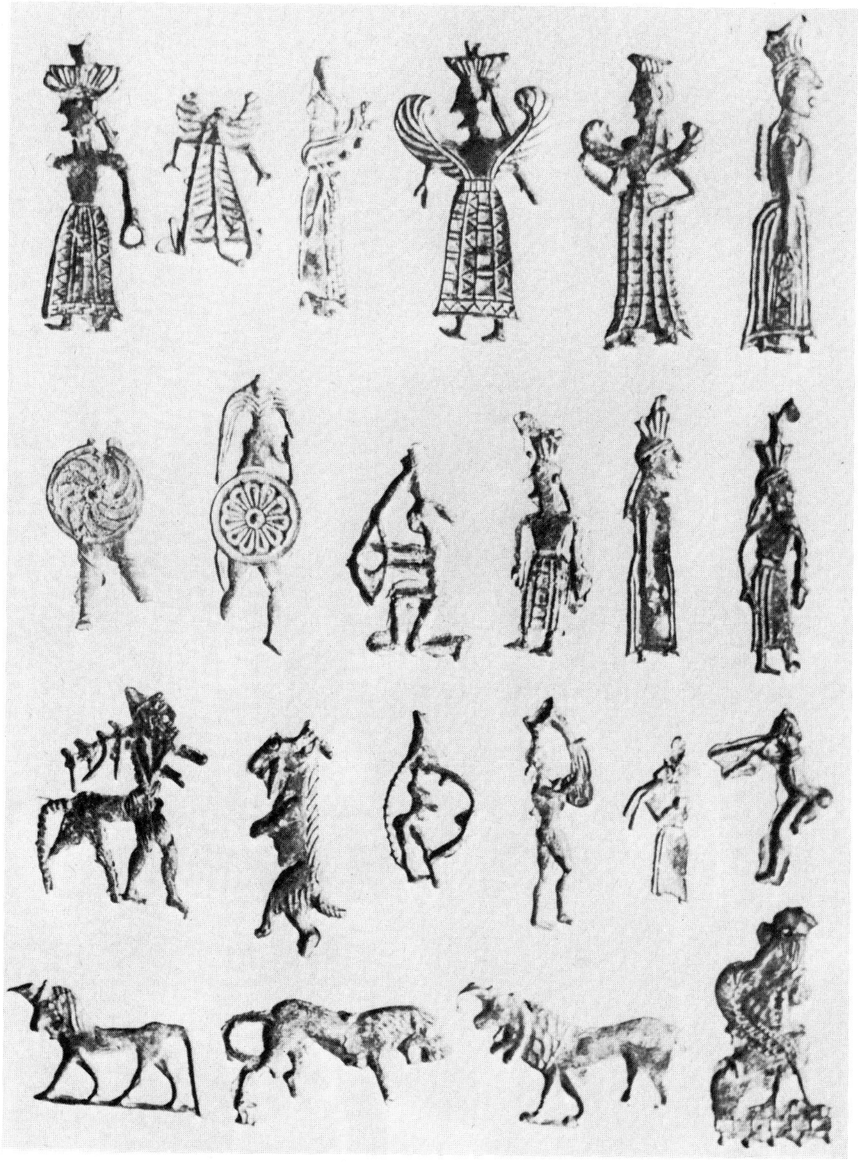

150 Lead I and II figurines from the temple of Orthia. Examples of these figurines are in a number of museums besides Sparta. Ht of tallest figure 5.5 cm

8

Miscellaneous Objects

Of the miscellaneous objects found at Sparta far the most numerous are the small lead votive reliefs. These were found at all levels from late Geometric to Hellenistic. The temple of Orthia alone yielded more than 100,000 and the Menelaeum several thousand; they were also found in smaller quantities at the Amyclaeum and at every other shrine, major or minor, excavated in the neighbourhood of Sparta. Only a few isolated examples have been found at other places in the Peloponnese, to which they were probably taken by visiting Spartans. The figures, from 2.5 to 8 cm (1 to 3 in.) high, were cast in shallow lead moulds which held several at a time. The backs were flat. They were obviously mass produced as the cheapest and most popular form of offering, something like the little medallions of saints that adorn wayside shrines and buses in modern Greece. There seems to be no significant difference between those dedicated at different shrines, but the predominant types and the number found at the Orthia site suggest that they were the product of a single factory working primarily for that temple and incidentally for others in the region. The following remarks will be based mainly on the Orthia finds.

The reliefs are classified according to the pottery with which they were found. In the Geometric strata (Lead o) they are rare (only 23 from the Orthia site) and confined to imitations of jewellery, with two sphinxes. They become frequent with Laconian I (Lead I, 5719 examples) and more so with Laconian II (Lead II, 9548 examples). In these periods copies of jewellery still predominate, but a number of figure types appear also. With Laconian III comes an almost complete change in the designs, even when the subjects are the same. The figures tend to be smaller and thinner. Jewellery patterns are fewer, and the number of other, especially human, types increases. Between Lead III and lead IV, as with the corresponding periods of pottery, there is no clear dividing line. This is the period of the lead figures' greatest popularity (Lead III–IV, 68,822 examples). After this they decline both in number and variety. Of Lead V, extending from the later sixth century down to the third quarter of the fifth, there were 10,617 examples; of Lead VI, from the late fifth century down to the third, 4773. By this time, too, the types are impoverished and stereotyped.

The quality of these figures is poor and their execution sketchy. They are of interest, however, for such insights as they may give us on the worship of the poorer people, including presumably non-Spartiates, who could afford only the cheapest offerings. Some may represent actual types from real life. In any case – and this may be their greatest interest – they present us with a vast gallery of iconographical elements, indisputably Spartan and approximately dated. Most, probably all, of the designs are derivative, crude copies of pieces of jewellery or carvings in costler materials of which in many cases they are the only remaining record.

Of divine figures the commonest in all periods is the winged nature goddess Orthia. In the earlier periods she is occasionally flanked by lions; more usually she carries a wreath. She wears the long Dorian gown, tightly belted and with linear patterns below the waist, and a high cap. Similar figures without wings may represent the goddess or human worshippers; they often carry a wreath and sometimes a pomegranate. In and after Lead III other, more conventional, deities are found. Now the goddess sometimes carries a bow, suggesting Artemis, and there are other figures representing Athena, Neptune and Hermes. The winged goddess, nevertheless, persists right to the end.

Of monsters, the favourite is the sphinx, first found in Lead O and continuing in various forms to Lead IV, but not later. The centaur, winged horse and gorgon are found, though rarely, in Lead I; sirens appear first in Lead II; none of these outlasts Lead IV. Among real animals, lions and horses are the most common. A goat climbing up a bush appears in Lead I, as do cocks; both become more common later. Bulls are added in Lead II, and deer are common from Lead III on, perhaps an indication that Artemis was taking over from Orthia, whose lion becomes rarer. Horse-head pendants, sometimes with a female figure between the heads, have a vogue in Lead II.

Of everyday human types easily the commonest is the armoured foot-soldier. He is already fully equipped in Lead I, with his crested helmet, round shield and greaves. His cuirass is hidden by his shield. He carries a short spear. One type, from

Lead II, shows him kneeling with shield held out to receive a charge. Archers are also shown, more frequently in the early periods, rarely in Lead III-IV. In Lead V a new type, with a more advanced kind of bow made from two pieces of horn, is again fairly common. In the early period the shields bear as devices rosettes or whirling rays, but in Lead III–IV the devices are a variety of gorgons, birds, animals and insects; the change is more probably due to imitation of vase painting than to any change in real life.

Apart from soldiers, there are from all periods musicians, male and female, with lyres or single or double pipes, with Lead III adding a cymbal-player. There are occasional revellers and runners or dancers, and from Lead III–IV rough figures of men walking, running or riding, either naked or wearing a short tunic. From Lead I comes an interesting bearded head in profile of sub-Geometric style, and also a miniature model of a mirror; from Lead II, as we should expect, a few examples of the Daedalic full-face female head. Otherwise the heads are regularly in profile in all periods, though the bodies may be represented frontally.

The imitation jewellery, at its most various in Lead II, confirms the impression given by the bronzes that personal adornment reached its peak in this period, and forms found in bronze, such as the bull's-head pendant, are copied in lead. Later than this, the jewellery is relatively less frequent and becomes stereotyped in form.

Inscriptions unfortunately give us little help. Frequent for the Hellenistic and still more for the Roman period, when the whole nature of the society had changed, they are sparse and uninformative for any time before the fourth century. Two public inscriptions of possibly fifth-century date have been found in Laconia; both may belong rather to the early fourth century. One, found in a church in central Laconia, is a list of contributors to a war fund. The other, recently discovered and apparently from the acropolis, contains a treaty with an otherwise unknown Aetolian people. In addition there are some half dozen inscriptions set up by the Spartan state elsewhere, mostly at Olympia.[1] The Spartan government did not have the habit of recording its laws on stone, a fact which is perhaps the origin of the story that Lycurgus forbad his laws to be written down. Nearly all the early private inscriptions are merely dedications, giving the name of the god and sometimes of the donor with an appropriate verb; some examples have been quoted in the chapter on sculpture.

The Laconian alphabet, used also in Messenia and Tarentum, is a special form of a family used in the western and central Peloponnese, in Phocis and Ozolian Locris in central Greece, in Thessaly in the north and in Rhodes in the east. Not all of these were Dorian. The most likely suggestion is that the alphabet was brought to Sparta from Delphi, and thence carried to Olympia. The oldest surviving Spartan inscription is the dedication to 'Helen the husband of Menelaus' neatly engraved on a bronze oil flask found at the Menelaeum in 1975 and dated by the shape of the flask to between 675 and 650.[2] Many of the carvings on soft limestone associated with the rebuilding of the temple of Orthia about 575 bear dedications probably cut by their makers; one, the torso of a horse, is signed 'Gareas made me'.[3] Another artist's signature, this time of the first quarter of the fifth century, is included with the dedication on a base from the shrine of Apollo Hyperteleatas at Feniki; it tells us that he was from Cyrene or that he was named 'the Cyrenean'.[4]

Towards the end of the sixth century there begins a series of longer inscriptions which continues through much of the fifth. These are slabs on which an individual records, by way of a dedication, his victories at various local games. They are mostly fragmentary and in some cases it is even doubtful whether they are victory lists, though this seems likely. The best preserved is the inscription which one Damonon dedicated to Athena Keeper of the City on the acropolis to commemorate the series of victories won by him and his son at festivals up and down Laconia and in near-by Argolis and Messenia 'such as no man of our time ever won', in chariot races and horse races with horses bred and driven or ridden by himself and in foot races over various distances.[5] These inscriptions are all neatly cut on slabs of local marble, and they testify to the growing interest in sport of well-to-do Spartans around this time, of which we have also literary evidence.

At the other end of the social scale, five inscriptions of roughly the same period from Cape Taenarum at the extreme southern point of Laconia record the manumission of slaves by means of formal dedication to Poseidon. These would be private slaves, not helots, but whether their masters were Spartiates or *perioeci* we do not know; more probably the latter.[6]

Outside Laconia, Olympia provides a few inscriptions of a more public character: the dedication of a bronze bowl in the first half of the sixth century, the inscription of the same period on a seat reserved for the Laconian Gorgos, official representative of Elis at Sparta, and finally the metrical dedication on the base of a bronze statue of Zeus 4 m (13 ft) high, requesting him to look favourably on the Lacedaemonians, dated on epigraphic grounds to the early years of the fifth century. The occasion, according to Pausanias, was a helot rising.[7]

To judge from the extant remains, the use of the precious metals was not common at Sparta at any time. A number of scraps of jewellery in gold, silver and silver gilt were found, mostly at the temple of Orthia and almost all with Laconian I or Laconian II pottery, but neither the quantity nor, except perhaps for a necklace of leaves and berries in gold and silver gilt of which only a few fragments survive, in quality are they remarkable. Gold seems mostly to have been used in the form of gold leaf to cover silver or even lead. Since such objects were likely to be kept for some time before they were dedicated, we may perhaps date their disuse to about the end of the seventh century, that is, to about the same time as the disuse of ivory, and attribute it to the same cause, the interruption of supplies by wars in Syria. So far as they go, the finds support the tradition of Spartan austerity, but it would be unwise to put much weight on such evidence.

Amber was fairly common in the Geometric period, but dropped out of use later, though it is occasionally found in conjunction with ivory or bone until the end of the sixth century. Imports had probably ceased much earlier. The iron spits, of which numerous much corroded fragments were found both at the temple of Orthia and on the acropolis, as well as a few on other Laconian sites, belong mostly to the first half of the seventh century, but are found occasionally as late as the third. Similar objects have been found elsewhere, notably at the Argive Heraeum. They do not seem to have had any connection with currency, but were perhaps for use in connection with the sacrifices of animals.

There remain to be mentioned a few objects from Egypt or Phoenicia, or perhaps Rhodian or Naucratite imitations of Egyptian articles. These consist of engraved stones and scarabs, vases and figures of vitreous paste; all were found in late Geometric or Laconian I contexts, and so belong to the middle and later seventh century. One of the vitreous paste figures, found with Laconian I, represents a naked woman of distinctly Egyptian appearance; she is perhaps the ancestor of the line of Laconian nude women.[8]

9
The Poets

Fairly extensive fragments have survived of the works of two seventh-century poets, Tyrtaeus and Alcman, who whether or not they were Spartan by birth were certainly so by adoption and interests.

Tyrtaeus wrote about the middle of the century, during and shortly after the second Messenian war. The Alexandrians had five books of his poems, containing martial exhortations, marching songs, and a poem known as *Eunomia* or 'Good Order'. We have three samples of the exhortations, one quoted by a fourth-century orator at Athens and two included in a late anthology, but only two quotations, totalling twelve lines, certainly from the *Eunomia*, and a few short quotations of uncertain source. There is also a papyrus, now in Berlin, on which are preserved about a dozen more or less complete lines and isolated words from another sixty lines. Two Spartan marching songs are quoted by later authors but their attribution to Tyrtaeus is doubtful.

Except for the songs, Tyrtaeus wrote in the elegiac metre evolved from the hexameter in Ionia a generation earlier, and in the Ionian dialect appropriate to that metre. Perhaps for this reason, as well as from reluctance to allow any poet to Sparta, Plato in the *Laws* calls him an Athenian who became a Spartan citizen,[1] and later a fable was elaborated that when the Messenian war was at first going badly the Spartans were advised by the Delphic oracle to seek a general from Athens. The Athenians, not wanting either to disobey the oracle or to see Sparta increase her power, sent in derision a lame schoolmaster, whose poems inspired the Spartans to victory. If we were to accept that this story had any basis, we might perhaps guess that Tyrtaeus was not a schoolmaster but a drill sergeant imported at the suggestion of the oracle to teach the Spartans the new technique of warfare the nearer exponents of which, such as Argos, were hostile. It is, however, more likely that he was a native Spartan, as an alternative tradition held.

However that may be, Tyrtaeus is our earliest and most explicit exponent of the practice and values of hoplite warfare, which, originating perhaps in the north-eastern Peloponnese about the beginning of the seventh century, was soon to spread all over Greece. In this, the chariot-borne noble with his motley following of men-at-arms was replaced by uniformly armoured infantry drawn up in close formation in a line several ranks deep. These soldiers were later known as hoplites; Tyrtaeus calls them *panoploi*, 'fully armoured men', and contrasts them with the *gymnetes*, unarmoured marksmen who covered the ends of the line from behind its shields. Each hoplite wore a bronze helmet with nose and cheek guards, a corselet with a turned-up rim above the hips, and greaves. On his left forearm he carried a round shield about 1 m (3 ft) in diameter, which covered the right side of the next man as well as its bearer, and in his right hand a long thrusting spear or pike which, with a sword for use in emergencies, was his only offensive weapon. The close wall of shields, bristling with spearpoints, was impenetrable as long as each man held his place; once it broke the men were exposed, hampered rather than helped by their heavy armour, and were an easy prey for the enemy – hence the great disparity in casualties between the two sides in most Greek battles. Battles became a kind of scrum, each side pushing until one of them gave way.

These tactics called for values quite different from those of the heroic battles of Homer or even of Callinus, Tyrtaeus's Ionian predecessor in patriotic elegiacs, who describes the good soldier as being regarded by his fellow-citizens as a demigod because he stands before their eyes 'like a tower', and 'does the work of many, though but one'.[2] In the hoplite battle there was no place for the aristocrat stepping out from the ranks to engage the enemy in single combat; the good soldier was the man who stood firm shoulder to shoulder as an equal member of a team. Not individual prowess and competition for glory, but steadiness and discipline, were needed.

Tyrtaeus's exhortations seem at first sight conventional and even commonplace. His vocabulary is almost entirely Homeric; hardly more than a score of words in more than 150 lines are not found in Homer, and stock epithets and metrical clichés abound, in a way that suggests that the dialect was learnt, not native. But a closer reading shows how by new combinations of familiar words and by subtle shifts of meaning Tyrtaeus is constantly inculcating values very different from those in his model, values of which his poems are the first surviving expression.

> 'Fear not the number of the enemy, nor be afraid, but let each man hold his shield straight towards the front . . . Of those who are bold enough to advance shoulder to shoulder to close quarters against the van of the enemy fewer are killed, and they save the folk behind, but all the merit of cowards is lost . . .
>
> 'It is easy to stab the fugitive in cruel war in the midriff from behind, and shameful is the corpse that lies in the dust with its wounds behind. So let a man stand firm, legs apart, and both feet rooted to the ground, biting his lip with his teeth, covering thighs and shins below and breast and shoulders in the hollow of his broad shield, and brandish his great spear in his right hand and shake the terrible crest above his head. Let him learn to fight by doing doughty deeds, and not stay out of range when he has a shield. Rather let him come close and taking one of the foe smite him hand to hand with great spear or sword, setting foot by foot and pressing shield to shield, bringing crest close to crest and helm to helm and breast to breast let him fight his man, grasping the hilt of his sword or his great spear'.[3]

In another poem Tyrtaeus expressly rejects the aristocratic ideals of physical excellence (such as that represented by the Olympic games, where Spartan victors had been frequent since the end of the first Messenian war), eloquence or wealth:

> 'I would not celebrate a man nor give him a place in my tale for speed of foot or wrestling, not though he had the stature and strength of the Cyclopes or beat the Thracian North Wind at running, not if he were lovelier of form than Tithonus or had greater riches than Midas or Cinyras, not if he were more kingly than Pelops Tantalus's son or more honeyed of tongue than Adrastus, not if he were famous for everything save stubborn courage; for no man is good in war unless he steels himself to the sight of bloody death and reaches out to smite the foe at close quarters.
>
> 'This is true merit, this the best prize among men and fairest for a young man to win. This is a common good for the city and all its people, when a man stands in the front line unyielding, putting shameful flight right out of his mind, staking his life and his enduring heart, and standing by the next man encourages him with his words. This is the good soldier, at once he turns to flight the rough ranks of the foe, and eagerly he stems the wave of battle.'[4]

War holds no glamour for Tyrtaeus. It is a grim business, as he shows in his graphic description of an old soldier 'whose joints are no longer supple', deserted by the younger men who should have covered him, lying with white hair and grizzled beard in the dust gasping out his life as he clutches at his bleeding groin.[5] Nor is there room for direct intervention of the gods; courage is something a man must impose on himself, not something inspired from outside, a function of his own character, not an accident.

The poem of which scraps are preserved on the Berlin papyrus is of different kind, less hortatory and more concrete and specific. It seems to be a speech delivered just before a battle, which is described in the future tense. In the more nearly complete portion we find the Spartans, fenced in by their hollow shields, with the three old Dorian tribes, Pamphyli, Hylleis and Dynames, drawn up separately, brandishing their ash-shafted spears. 'Putting all our trust in the immortal gods', we are told, 'we will obey our leaders.' Spearmen and others will attack all together, and when the battle is joined there will be a 'dreadful din' as shields clash on shields, spears are deflected by breastplates and bronze helmets clang to the blows of great stones. This is not a hoplite battle, but a good old-fashioned mêlée, though some of the elements of what was to become hoplite armour are used. In one of the mutilated lines a chariot is mentioned. There are two references to a wall and one to a tower, which suggests that the action is not a pitched battle but an assault on a fortified place. Another line identifies the enemy as Messenians, but there is no way in which we can tell what the context was or which war was referred to. Some have identified the speaker with Tyrtaeus himself in the capacity of a Spartan general, but this is not necessary, and the speech could be a dramatic interpolation in the narrative of an incident of the first war.[6]

The occasion of the *Eunomia*, Aristotle tells us, was a time of civil unrest associated with the war and concerned with the distribution of land, probably of the reconquered Messenian plain. The title does not suggest a blueprint for constitutional reform, but rather a plea for right behaviour and a right attitude to the state, for 'law and order' as a modern conservative might say. We have too little of the poem to be sure of its drift, but the plea seems to have been backed by appeals to religion and to history. One fragment tells how 'Zeus himself, the son of Cronos and husband of fair-garlanded Hera, gave this town to the

Heracleidae, with whom we left windy Erineus and came to the broad isle of Pelops', Erineus being a mountain in Doris in central Greece. The next line seems to have referred to Athena.[7] The well-known quotations referring to the first Messenian war may well also come from this poem. In the first of these credit for the conquest of 'Messene good to plough and good to sow' is given to 'our king, beloved of the gods, Theopompus', and we are told that 'about it fought for nineteen years, relentlessly, keeping ever a patient heart, the spearmen, our fathers' fathers', and in the twentieth year the Messenians 'abandoning their rich fields fled from the great mountains of Ithome'.[8] The other two extracts describe some of the results. The Messenians 'oppressed like asses with great burdens' were forced to bring to their masters half of all their crop, and, with their wives, to mourn for them when they died.[9] The first quotation emphasizes the role in the original conquest of King Theopompus and of the spearmen ancestors of the hoplites of the second war. The other two perhaps refer to the greed and arrogance of the aristocrats who partitioned the plain among themselves and exploited its resources in a semi-feudal style, so bringing about the rebellion. The mourning exacted of the tenants was like that of the Spartans for their kings,[10] and the Messenians were reduced not to helots who paid a fixed amount for the upkeep of their master, but to share farmers or 'half-and-halfers'.

Certainly from the *Eunomia* is the extract which purports to give the authority of the Delphic oracle to a brief description of the machinery for reaching public decisions and the part in it of the three 'estates' of the community:

> 'Having heard the voice of Phoebus they brought home from Pytho the oracles of the god and words which must be fulfilled. First in counsel shall be the kings, honoured by the gods, whose care is the lovely city of Sparta, and the aged elders; after them the men of the commons, obeying the right rules, shall say what is fair and do all that is just, and not counsel aught crooked for the city. Then victory and power shall follow the people. For so did Phoebus reveal to the city concerning these matters.'[11]

The kings are given two lines; the elders are dismissed almost as an afterthought in two words, both emphasizing that age is their qualification, not birth or property. The second word, *geron*, while it is the common word for 'old man', may already have the technical sense of a member of the *gerousia* or Spartan senate, but we are not told how many they were or how they were chosen. After these, the 'men of the commons' (the epithet appearing here for the first time), no doubt the new class of hoplites brought into being by the war, is guaranteed a voice, but subject to strict limitations of which the precise meaning is not clear. The hexameter lines may contain the original oracle, the alternating pentameters being paraphrase or gloss on them. As we should expect in an oracle, or a moral exhortation, there is a lack of specific detail, in marked contrast with the 'Great Rhetra' (to be discussed later) which Plutarch quotes alongside this passage.

From these few fragments it is impossible to reconstruct the *Eunomia* in detail. We can see that Tyrtaeus was a strong supporter of the monarchy, which he invests with religious sanction and in which he perhaps saw a bulwark against the pretensions of the aristocracy. He seems to minimize the place of the nobles, and gives a small but definite place to the new hoplite class. Just as he used Homeric language to cover the new message of the martial poems, so here his account is basically conservative, differing only in emphasis from the customary assembly of kings, counsellors and commons found in Homer. It may be significant that the word *polis*, in the new sense of a political community formed around a geographical centre with a common body of religious and historical associations, appears three times in the ten lines of the account of the Delphic oracle; this concept perhaps provided the centre for loyalty and unity which in war had been provided by the hoplite line. It is significant that neither here nor, we may be certain, elsewhere, did Tyrtaeus mention Lycurgus; had he done so the reference could not have escaped the notice of later writers like Plutarch, desperate for any scrap of authentication for that elusive character.

If Tyrtaeus is the poet of 'barrack Sparta', the familiar Sparta of the later tradition in shaping which his poems played an important part, Alcman depicts the other 'swinging Sparta', care-free, beauty-loving, with wide intellectual interests and geographical horizons.[12] The contradiction used to be explained by supposing Alcman to be earlier than Tyrtaeus, as some later chronologers said he was, and that he represented a short-lived burst of prosperity following the original conquest of Messenia, while Tyrtaeus expressed the narrow militarism evoked by the second war and never thereafter relaxed. But a recently discovered fragment of a commentary on Alcman shows that he mentioned King Leotychidas, who reigned in the last part of the seventh century.[13] This fits an alternative traditional date, 610 BC, and is also more consistent with the archaeology. Tyrtaeus will then be contemporary with the austere style of Laconian I pottery and the early Daedalic reliefs, as well as with the first representation of a hoplite in Lead I, while Alcman coincides with the more exuberant pottery, abundance of personal ornaments in ivory and bronze and expanding exports of Laconian II.

Alcman was best known for his Maiden Songs, choruses to be sung and danced by choirs of girls at festivals of the gods and goddesses of Sparta. A large part of one of these has fortunately been preserved on papyrus; apart from this and a much shorter fragment discovered more recently, he is known to us only in short extracts, ranging from a single word to a few lines, quoted by later scholars not for their content or poetic merit, but to illustrate unusual words or grammatical or metrical usages. We know that in addition to Maiden Songs he wrote other types of hymn for male choirs and single voices, and perhaps also preludes for public recitations of Homer and drinking songs. All of his work was intended for public performance by choirs or groups, and we must be cautious about reading autobiographical references into them, expecially as we do not know the context of the fragments we have. Alcman took seriously his role as a public spokesman inspired by the Muses and the songs of the birds; unlike earlier poets he often names himself, especially in the less solemn fragments.

Sparta had already a tradition of religious music and poetry to which poets from Lesbos, Crete and Ionia had contributed. In addition, Alcman was familiar with Homer, and also with the Boeotian school of cosmological epic of which the Hesiodic *Theogony* is an example, and he drew on both for subject-matter and vocabulary. He was also a teacher of the new morality currently being spread from Delphi of restraint towards the gods and simplicity in daily life. He wrote not, like Tyrtaeus, in an imported literary language, but basically in the local Dorian dialect, to which he gave new breadth and poetic respectability while still keeping in touch with the colloquial language of the people. He was fond of unusual words, whether names of plants or dishes or of exotic places; a late scholar wrote a treatise in two books on place-names in Alcman. This, together with his condensed and allusive style and the loss of the performance and ritual of which the poems formed part made him difficult even to later Greeks and a mine of examples for grammarians and lexicographers.

The range of Alcman's matter is as diverse as his language. He liked legends with a Laconian setting which linked his audience to the heroic world of pre-Dorian Greece, but he also retold stories from Homer such as that of Odysseus and Nausicaa, of which the romantic possibilities perhaps appealed to him. He took from Hesiod the trick of summing up a story in a pithy moral generalization, and also of expressing the connection between abstract concepts in genealogical form, while in another mood he would use the language of the common people, with whom he liked to identify himself, and their proverbial sayings.

Above all, he was a keen and close observer of things around him, of the ritual dances with their costumes brilliant with gold, silver and purple, of the golden or auburn hair and well-turned ankles of the girls, of midnight Dionysiac revels or simple meals. He was a lover of nature, and birds and flowers abound in his poems and his imagery. Nausicaa's maids, when Odysseus bursts from the thicket among them, 'sink helpless, like birds when a hawk hovers over them'.[14] Possibly referring to his own old age, he recalls the legend of the kingfisher who, when too old to fly, is carried by the hens on their wings:

> 'No more, maidens honey tongued, of holy voice, can my limbs bear me. Would, ah would I were a kingfisher, who skims over the flower of the wave with the halycons, keeping a dauntless heart, the sea-blue sacred bird.'[15]

But his best-known piece in this vein is the description of the stillness of night over Taygetus:

> 'Now sleep the mountain peaks and the ravines, ridges and torrent streams, all creeping things that black night nourishes, wild upland beasts and the race of bees and monsters in the gulfs of the dark-gleaming sea; now sleep the tribes of long-winged birds'.[16]

The conventions of the Maiden Song allowed an interlude of banter, couched in the language of love, between members of the chorus and their leader, and it is to a misunderstanding of such passages by scholars, ignorant of the conditions of performance and more accustomed to personal poetry, that Alcman owed his later reputation as the founder of Greek love poetry and himself of loose life. A good example is found in a fragment recently published from a papyrus from Oxyrhynchus. Though the text is imperfect, the erotic character of the language is clear:

> 'With how melting a glance does she look towards me, more tender than sleep and death; nor are such sweets idly proffered. But Astymeloisa answers me not, but wearing her garland like some bright star shooting across the sky or golden sprout or soft plume she strides with feet outstretched . . . grace sits on the maiden's tresses . . . Were she but to look at me . . . coming close to hold me with her soft hand, quickly would I become her suppliant.[17]

This looks like the language of passionate love, but it means no more than similar language addressed, through the chorus, to Hagesichora or Agido or Megalostrata or Clesimbrota.[18] It tells us nothing of the poet's personal life, but much of the society, gay, aristocratic and uninhibited, in which such language was current and such banter possible.

We come perhaps nearer to Alcman himself in his references to food, though these are also a concrete expression of his advocacy of simplicity of life. One fragment describes the preparations for a party:

> 'Seven couches and as many tables crowned with poppy-seed loaves and linseed and sesame, and among the cups dishes of honey-cake.'[19]

Another praises the fragrance of the several local vintages of six villages in various parts of Laconia. But Alcman dissociates himself, by name, from any fancy for unusual or elaborate food. In a fragment accompanying the presentation of a vessel, perhaps as a prize in some contest, he wrote:

> 'And sometime I shall give you a three-legged cauldron in which to prepare your dinner. As yet it is unfired, but soon it will be full of lentil soup, such as all-devouring Alcman loves hot after the winter solstice. For he eats not daintily prepared food, but craves for common dishes, like the people.'[20]

References to distinctively Spartan institutions are few and of uncertain significance. The claim that 'good lyre-playing takes precedence over (or rivals) iron'[21] might be a protest against the encroachment of military values in peacetime, but might equally be no more than a claim of status by the poet. Similarly the description of Order (*Eunomia*) as daughter of Forethought and sister of Fortune and Persuasion[22] might be an aristocratic alternative to Tyrtaeus's more authoritarian concept of Order as resting on the divine right of the kings, but might be no more than an exercise in genealogical description. Two fragments mention the common meals, but neither uses the technical names by which these were later known, nor suggests their central function in 'Lycurgan' Sparta; in both cases they might be no more than conservative dinner-clubs surviving from primitive times with a social rather than military function. In one, some unidentified person is said to be 'mourned at the mill and at the common suppers'[23] where the general meaning is clearly 'by high and low'. The expression is colloquial and perhaps proverbial; the word for the common meal is compounded from a dialect word for 'supper' which is used elsewhere by Alcman for a meal he was preparing for himself. The second reference: 'at feasts and ceremonies in the mess it is proper to raise the paean',[24] the paean being a kind of hymn for male voices, originally in honour of Apollo, but also sung going into battle. The word translated 'mess' (*andreion* or 'men's meal') survived in Crete and was, we are told, the earlier name for the Spartan *syssition*. It probably represents a primitive Dorian custom, without the military overtones acquired later.

Alcman is best represented by the Maiden Song of the Paris papyrus, of which the second half is almost complete, while enough remains of the first half to allow a reconstruction of its general contents. There have been a number of explanations of the poem, and in the absence of the music, dance and ritual that accompanied it much of the detail must remain uncertain; but there is a substantial area of agreement. What follows is based mainly on the discussions of Page and Bowra.

The occasion was a dawn ceremony at the time of the spring solstice, when the Pleiads and the sun rise at the same time, and the purpose was to avert evil from the crops for which ploughing was about to begin. Bowra has argued convincingly that the deity invoked was Helen, whom we know to have been worshipped at Sparta as a vegetation goddess. The poem was sung by a choir of ten girls, divided into two sections, one led by Hagesichora, who was also leader of the whole, and one by Agido. The girls would be chosen from the daughters of prominent families; Hagesichora may have been connected with the Agiad kings. There is no evidence that competition with another choir was involved.

The chorus probably began with a short invocation to the Muses, after which the first half narrated the legend of the slaying of the sons of Hippocoon, king of Sparta and brother of

Tyndareus, the human father of Helen and the Dioscuri. In later versions the sons of Hippocoon were killed by Heracles in a personal quarrel; in Alcman the Dioscuri were also involved. The narrative was followed by a solemn warning against presumption:

> 'Destiny and Contrivance, oldest of the gods, destroyed them, and vain was their might. Let none of mankind soar to heaven, nor seek to wed Aphrodite, the Cyprian queen, nor any fair daughter of Porcus the sea god. The Graces whose glances dart love enter the house of Zeus.'

This was followed by a short account of the battle of the gods and the giants, the moral of which serves as the transition to the second part of the poem.

> 'Unforgettable things did they suffer, for they plotted evil. There is vengeance of the gods. Blessed is the man who happily weaves the day without a tear.'

Then the chorus divides into parts and its members engage in direct personalities and banter, while, we must imagine, the leaders perform the ritual acts required of them.

> 'But I sing the light of Agido; I see her like the sun, upon whose brightness she calls for us. But our glorious leader forbids me to praise her or blame; for to us she seems pre-eminent, as though one were to set among the grazing beasts a colt, sturdily built, a champion with thundering hooves, the stuff of winged dreams.
>
> 'Do you not see? The one is a Venetic courser, but the hair of my niece Hagesichora blooms like pure gold; and of her silvery face why should I speak to you openly? She is Hagesichora! Second to her the beauty of Agido runs like a Colaxaean steed against one of the Ibenian stock. For the Pleiads at dawn, rising through the ambrosial dark like the star Sirius, fight against us as we bring the plough. Neither is such abundance of purple enough to ward off evil from us, nor speckled snake of solid gold, nor Lydian headband, adornment of soft-eyed girls, nor Nanno's hair nor the divine beauty of Areta, nor Syllacis nor Klessistera; not though you go to Aenesimbrota's place and say: "Give me Astaphis, and let Phylylla look upon me and Damareta and lovely Wianthemis." But Hagesichora protects me; for is not fair-ankled Hagesichora here with us? She stands near Agido and

> praises our festival. Receive her prayers, ye gods; for to the gods belong the achievement and the end. Choir-leader, to you would I say, I am but a girl that shrieks to no effect like an owl on a rafter. But I long to please the Dawn Goddess, for she is the healer of our troubles; through Hagesichora the girls have attained the peace they love. For a chariot must follow the trace-horse; and on a ship the pilot must be obeyed. She is not more tuneful than the Sirens, for they are goddesses, and instead of eleven we are but ten girls singing. Yet it sounds like a swan by the streams of Xanthus. She with her yellow hair . . . .' (the last four lines are lost).[25]

There were other Spartan poets, and we know the names of some of them, though all their work is lost: Dionysodotus whose paeans were sung with those of Alcman at the Festival of Unarmed Boys (*Gymnopaedia*) at Amyclae; Spendon, performance of whose choruses, like those of Terpander and Alcman, was forbidden to helots in the fourth century; and Gitiadas, bronze-worker and architect of the temple of Athena on the acropolis, who wrote songs in the Dorian dialect, including a hymn to the goddess.[26] All these were probably later than Alcman; Gitiadas belongs to the middle of the sixth century. After this, original poetry was no longer written at Sparta. In the fifth century literature, like sculpture, became professional and pan-Hellenic, and the tradition of choral lyric with its roots in local cult was taken over by a new school of poets, often working for private patrons, in which Spartans had no place.

The old songs and rituals were still carefully preserved and performed, and Sparta could still be called, in an epigram celebrating Lysander's victory over Athens at Aegospotamae in 405, the 'land of lovely choirs' as well as 'the citadel of Greece'.[27] Aristophanes, in the pastiche sung by the Spartan delegates as the final chorus of the *Lysistrata*, shows the maiden dances still performed at the end of the fifth century as in the days of Alcman:

> O to watch her bonnie dochters
> Sport along Eurotas' waters!
> Winsome feet for every plyin',
> Fleet as fillies, wild an' gay,
> Winsome tresses tossin', flyin',
> As o' Bacchanals at play.
> Leda's dochter, on before us,
> Pure and sprety, guides the Chorus.[28]

10
Through Foreign Eyes

It was not a Spartan, but Simonides of Ceos, the first of the professional poets, who composed the dirge for those killed in the battle of Thermopylae to be sung at a shrine, probably at Sparta, where they were to be worshipped as heroes. Nine lines survive; their studied antitheses and emotional rhythm are characteristic of the new style:

> 'Of those that died at Thermopylae glorious is the fortune, beautiful the fate; for a tomb they have an altar, for lamentation remembrance, for pity praise. Their memorial neither mould nor all-conquering death can tarnish. This shrine of brave men has for guardian the honour of Hellas; witness too is Leonidas, Sparta's king, who has left behind a great model of excellence and everlasting fame.'[1]

For the other Greeks Simonides wrote the epitaph for their grave at Thermopylae; 'O stranger, take word to the Lacedaemonians that we lie here obedient to their words.'[2]

Sparta reached the peak of her glory with Thermopylae in 480, and of her power with the surrender of Athens in 404. Between these dates our internal sources fail. There was no Spartan poet after the sixth century, no prose writer, if we except a pamphlet by the exiled king Pausanias, until the antiquary Sosibius at the beginning of the third century. Even the archaeological remains are meagre and uninspiring. Henceforth we see Sparta only through the eyes of outsiders, limited by the information at their disposal and by their preconceptions and purposes.

To this, Herodotus is a partial exception. He gathered much of his information about Sparta during a visit made in the course of his researches, sometimes checking or supplementing it from other sources. Himself cosmopolitan and a pan-Hellenist by conviction, he was also a good oral historian who made it his business, as he tells us, to report faithfully what was said whether he himself believed it all or not.[3] The result is a conspectus of so much of the history current at Sparta in the middle of the fifth century as Herodotus thought relevant to his wider theme of the conflict between Greece and Persia and its antecedents on both sides of the Aegean.

The stories gathered by Herodotus fall into two groups; legendary tales explaining something in the present but set in an indeterminate past defined only by reference to other legendary events, and historical narratives dealing with events falling within about three generations of Herodotus's own time, when material passed on by parents and grandparents would still be fresh in the memory of his informants. Between the ninth century and the sixth Spartan history is for Herodotus virtually a blank. The nearer the events the fuller the detail is likely to be, and the greater the chance of political distortion.

Herodotus describes the rise of Spartan power up to the Persian invasions of Greece in three episodes. The first is linked to the Persian conquest of Lydia in 546, the second to the Persian expedition against Egypt in 525 and the affairs of Polycrates of Samos, and the third, which is in two parts, to the revolt of the Ionian Greeks against Persia in 499 and the demand for 'earth and water' as a prelude to the invasion of Greece in 491.

In the first episode, Croesus of Lydia sent envoys to Greece to seek allies against the rising power of Persia. They learnt that Sparta had lately become the leading power on the Peloponnese, having emerged victorious from a long struggle with Tegea begun in the previous generation. 'Even before this', Herodotus was told, the Spartans had been 'the worst organized internally of all the Greeks, and with no foreign contacts', but had been brought to good order by Lycurgus, a Spartan of repute whom the Delphic oracle was uncertain whether to call a man or a god, but inclined to think him a god. According to one story the oracle then dictated to him the whole Spartan system, but the Spartans themselves said he brought it from Crete. As regent for his nephew Leobotas he 'changed all their customs', instituting not only their military organization and common messes, but also the ephors and elders. When he died, the Spartans paid him divine honours, and from that time prospered in all they did until land-hunger and an ambiguous oracle led them to try to annex the Tegean plain.

Victory was followed, not by annexation but by an extension of Spartan influence. The Spartans accepted the alliance with Croesus, to whom they were already under an obligation for a generous gift of gold for a statue of Apollo, and to seal it they had a large bronze mixing bowl decorated with reliefs made to send to him, but Sardis fell while it was on its way and it was diverted, either by sale or by piracy, to Samos, where it was dedicated at the temple of Hera. When Croesus was besieged and sent for help, the Spartans were at war with Argos for the control of Cynuria, and by the time they had won the battle of Thyrea and prepared ships it was too late. An appeal from the Greeks of Asia Minor was rejected, but the Spartans sent an ultimatum to Cyrus forbidding him to harm any Greek city, which was treated with contempt.[4]

The next episode concerned Sparta's relations with Samos. Polycrates sent a number of suspected opponents in 525 with forty triremes to help Cambyses in Egypt, but instead they came to Sparta and sought help to depose the tyrant. The Spartans sent an expedition to Samos, their first to Asian waters, but it returned unsuccessful; Herodotus dismisses as 'a rather silly story' a rumour that its leaders had been bribed with lead coins specially minted by Polycrates. After the capture of Samos by the Persians, Polycrates's successor Maeandrius came to Sparta for help and tried to bribe the new king, Cleomenes, who had him expelled by the ephors lest he should find some other Spartan more corruptible.[5]

Next comes a purely legendary interlude, linking Thera and through it Cyrene with Sparta. Some descendants of the Argonauts came to Sparta, where they were given land and citizenship. When they claimed to share in the kingship and did 'other unholy things' they were driven out except one family, the Aigiadae; some of them colonized Thera, which was re-named after their leader.[6] Thera in turn sent colonists to Cyrene.

The last historical episode or group of episodes centres around Cleomenes, to whom Aristagoras of Miletus appealed for help in the Ionian revolt. Cleomenes is now formally introduced, as if he had just come to the throne, with a long account of the circumstances of his birth and of his youth and the adventures of his half-brother Dorieus. Like Maeandrius, Aristagoras tried to bribe him, but he is saved by the timely intervention of his eight-year-old daughter who happened to be in the room.

Aristagoras went on to Athens, where he was more successful. Eleven years before, Cleomenes had led a Spartan force which had helped to drive the tyrant Hippias from Athens. Later, attempting to intervene in favour of the oligarchic faction against the Alcmaeonids he was shut up in the Acropolis and forced to capitulate, and two subsequent attempts to embroil Sparta and her allies in a full-scale war with Athens had been thwarted by the other king, Demaratus, and Corinth. Some scholars have suggested, though Herodotus does not say so, that the oligarchic party was temporarily in the ascendant at Athens and that Cleomenes sent Aristagoras to them for help which he knew Sparta would not give.[7]

We now move on to 491, with the Persian invasion imminent. Aegina, blocking the entrance to the Piraeus, had submitted to Darius, and the Athenians appealed to Sparta. Cleomenes took a Spartan force to Aegina to secure hostages, but the intrigues of Demaratus prevented him from doing so. Here Herodotus introduces the legendary story of the origin of the dual kingship and the rivalry of the two royal houses, and describes the privileges of the Spartan kings in war and peace and certain other Spartan customs.

On his return from Aegina Cleomenes conspired with Leotychidas, a distant cousin of Demaratus and next in line for the throne, to rake up an old scandal about his birth and have him deposed. Cleomenes, accompanied by Leotychidas, went back to Aegina and took hostages, whom he handed over to Athens. Demaratus went into voluntary exile at the Persian court.

Later, the friends of Demaratus forced Cleomenes to leave Sparta in disgrace. After spending some time in Thessaly he went to Arcadia and tried to unite the Arcadian cities against Sparta. He was recalled to Sparta and, according to Herodotus, went mad and committed suicide by slashing himself with a knife. Herodotus attributes this to his treatment of Demaratus, but others said it was due to his sacrilege in a war a few years earlier against Argos, when, after defeating the Argive army at Sepeia, near Tiryns, he had burnt the survivors in a sacred grove where they had taken refuge. On his return, he had been accused of taking bribes not to attack Argos itself, but was acquitted. After Cleomenes's death Leotychidas was given up to the Aeginetans and sent by them to Athens to secure the return of the hostages, which, however, he failed to do. Some time later he was exiled for taking bribes while on an expedition in Thessaly.[8]

In a later passage explaining the presence of a Plataean contingent at Marathon, Herodotus mentions incidentally that Cleomenes, happening to be with a Spartan force in central Greece, had referred the Plataeans to Athens for protection against Thebes; according to Thucydides this was in 519.[9]

Herodotus's sources were strongly biased against Cleomenes. He is said to have been unbalanced from his youth, to have owed his throne to birth, not merit, and to have reigned for only a short time, though in Herodotus's own account the events of his reign span nearly thirty years! His actions are attributed to spite or to insane ambition, and he was alleged to have exerted pressure on the Delphic oracle for his own ends. He is compared unfavourably with Dorieus and even with the medizing Demaratus. Yet he clearly fascinated Herodotus, and dominates the latter's account of Sparta in the years before the Persian invasion as he dominated Sparta itself. Ever since, his motives have been controversial. Some modern historians see in the actions recorded by Herodotus evidence of a far-sighted anticipation of the threat from Persia and a consistent attempt to organize Greece under Spartan hegemony to resist it. Others, among them Herodotus, see only personal motives. An anti-Persian motive is clear in the exaction of hostages from Aegina, and perhaps in the pre-emptive war with Argos a little earlier. Before this, it is more doubtful, though with hindsight his attempts to establish influence in Athens and even his presence in central Greece in 519 can be seen as consistent with it.

The career of Cleomenes brings us to the brink of the Persian invasions which are Herodotus's central theme. In the first campaign of 490 Sparta played no part; Cleomenes was in exile. When the Persians landed and Athens sent an urgent plea for help, a religious scruple prevented the Spartans from marching before the full moon; they arrived, after covering 150 miles in three days, the day after the battle of Marathon.[10]

In spite of this, when the much greater invasion came in 480, Sparta was unanimously accepted as leader of the Greek forces on both land and sea, though Athens contributed by far the largest fleet and, in Themistocles, the most active and committed leader. At sea, the credit of defeating the Persians went to Athens, the Spartan admiral being depicted as alternately bribed and cajoled by Themistocles; but on land the battle of Thermopylae was Sparta's alone, and in that of Plataea she played the principal part.

The story of Thermopylae is one of Herodotus's best known passages. The Spartans were again celebrating a festival, but they sent an advance party of three hundred chosen Spartiates and four thousand allies under Leonidas, Cleomenes's half-brother and successor, to hold the pass of Thermopylae while the fleet at Artemiseum defended the adjoining strait. For two days successive waves of attackers broke on the pass in vain. Then a local Greek took the Persians by night over a mountain track to take the Greeks in the rear. On the third morning Leonidas sent home all but the Spartans and two small allied contingents, one of doubtful loyalty. Towards noon the Persians attacked from both front and rear:

> 'So the barbarians with Xerxes advanced, and the Greeks with Leonidas, like men marching out to die, came much further out than before into the wider part of the pass . . . And knowing that death was inevitable because of the force that had gone round the mountain, they put forth all their strength against the barbarians, careless of life and utterly reckless. By now most of their spears were broken and they were hacking at the Persians with their swords. And Leonidas fell in the thick of it, showing himself the bravest of men, and with him other Spartans of renown, whose names I found out as men well deserving it, and I found out the names of all the three hundred.'[11]

Two Spartans were behind the lines blinded by ophthalmia. One ordered his helot to lead him to the battle and was killed; the other returned to Sparta to find himself disgraced and shunned, but redeemed himself by an honourable death at Plataea. A third, who had been sent away with a message and missed the battle, committed suicide.

A chorus is provided by speeches put into the mouth of the exiled Demaratus, now with Xerxes in Greece. At the Hellespont he warned Xerxes that he was about to meet the finest soldiers in the world, for though free men, they had a master, custom, which they feared more than his subjects did him. 'They do what it commands, and its command is always the same, never to flee from any number of men, but to stand firm in their ranks and win or die.' Before the battle he explains to the king that it is the habit of the Spartans to groom their hair before risking their lives, and after it he warns the king that there were eight thousand men in Sparta, each as good as the men who had fought in the battle; the other Lacedaemonians, though not their equals, were still good soldiers. He advised the king not to try to force the Isthmus, but to send his fleet to occupy Cythera and attack Laconia from the sea, recalling a saying of Chilon, 'the wisest of the Spartans', that it would be better for Sparta if Cythera were sunk below the sea.[12]

Thermopylae was the Spartan myth incarnate. What had been till then the ideal of a party was displayed to all Greece. After this the battle of Plataea, by which in the following year the Persians were driven out of Greece for ever, could only be an anticlimax. This time the allies were out in full strength, including five thousand Spartans and as many hoplites from the *perioeci*, with thirty-five thousand helots equipped as light troops. Pausanias, a nephew of Leonidas and regent for his young son, was commander-in-chief. The confused manoeuvres before the battle, and especially the insubordination of a Spartan officer who refused to withdraw to a better position because 'he would not bring disgrace on Sparta', show already the danger of a myth too literally believed. Pausanias's conduct after the battle was typical of a chivalrous Greek aristocrat rather than of a Spartan officer, and his inscription of his own name on the allied dedication at Delphi was resented at Sparta, and was the first step in his downfall.[13]

On the same day as Plataea the Greek fleet under king Leotychidas defeated the Persian navy off Mycale in Asia Minor. Considering the war finished, Leotychidas went home, leaving the liberation of the Greeks of the islands and Asia to Athens.[14]

Of Spartan institutions, only the dual monarchy seemed to Herodotus so unusual as to warrant special explanation. The elders are mentioned directly only twice, the ephors half a dozen times in various contexts without their functions being discussed, though some increase in their powers can be traced, perhaps as a reaction to the arbitrary conduct of Cleomenes. The helots are likewise shown without comment as the lowest stratum of Spartan society, serving as light troops at Marathon and Plataea (at the latter outnumbering the Spartans by seven to one, if Herodotus is to be believed), acting as a labour corps to collect the spoils at Plataea or firewood to burn out the Argive fugitives at Sepeia, or occasionally as personal servants to the invalid soldier at Thermopylae or to the mad Cleomenes.

To Herodotus the Spartans were first and foremost Greeks, ranged with other Greeks against the alien civilization of Asia. No summary can do justice to the richness and variety of his narrative, which is full of sidelights on Spartan life. We are told at length of the matrimonial affairs of the kings Anaxandridas and Ariston, fathers respectively of Cleomenes and Demaratus. The first refused to divorce his wife, whom he loved, at the bidding of the ephors because she was childless, and became the only Spartan ever allowed to have two wives and households at once. That the first wife was his niece and the second probably of Chilon's family suggests political undercurrents not mentioned by Herodotus. Ariston, on the other hand, fell madly in love with his best friend's wife and having tricked his friend into giving her up married her himself, divorcing his own wife, also for childlessness. Demaratus in his own turn married the betrothed of his cousin Leotychidas, also of Chilon's family, thus making an enemy for the future.

Women play a frequent part in Herodotus's Spartan tales; for example Gorgo, Cleomenes's eight-year-old daughter, is playing in the room while her father discusses affairs of state with Aristagoras, and later, now the wife of Leonidas, showed how to decode the secret warning from Demaratus of Xerxes's decision to invade Greece. Or there is the baby so ugly that her nurse took her every day up to the Menelaeum to pray before the image of Helen that she might be delivered from her ugliness. One day as they were leaving the temple a woman appeared and asked the nurse what she was carrying. When the nurse reluctantly unwrapped the baby, the woman stroked her head and foretold that she would grow to be the most beautiful woman in Sparta; so indeed she did, and became the wife of king Ariston.

Another side of Spartan life appears in the story of Glaucus, renowned for his honesty, with whom a Milesian stranger left a large sum of money for safekeeping. When many years later the Milesian's sons claimed the money and produced the agreed token, Glaucus asked the Delphic oracle whether he might swear falsely to keep the money. He was told that in the eyes of the god the thought was as bad as the deed, and though he returned the money, two generations later his line was extinct. Finally, there is the picture of the Spartan soldiers practising athletics and combing their long hair in front of the wall at Thermopylae. The Spartans, like the other Greeks, were a superstitious people and much addicted to oracles, especially that of Delphi, but Sparta as seen by Herodotus was a very human place.

The works of other historians of Herodotus's generation have been lost, but surviving fragments show that there was not yet a standard account of Spartan history. Simonides made Lycurgus a member of the Eurypontid family, not, like Herodotus, of the Agiad, and his version was commonly followed. Hellanicus of Lesbos did not mention Lycurgus, but ascribed the Spartan system to the first two kings, Eurysthenes and Proclus; Pindar implied that it was even older, praising Sparta for having kept unchanged the laws of Aegimius, the legendary ancestor of the Dorians.[15] Antiochus of Syracuse, who wrote a history of the Greek settlements in Italy, probably drew on local tradition which would have been transmitted independently of Sparta since the eighth century, for his account of the foundation of Tarentum in which he says that those Lacedaemonians who did not take part in the first Messenian war 'were condemned to slavery and called helots'; children born during the absence of the army were refused citizenship, and when they grew up they founded Tarentum.[16]

Thucydides's theme was the war between Athens and Sparta from 431 to 404, the greatest war and the most far-reaching in its effects up to his time. His purpose was to help to understand the future, to produce 'a work of permanent value, not a prize essay for immediate pleasure'. For him Sparta is the antagonist of Athens, and this is naturally the aspect emphasized. But if Thucydides leaves a very different impression of Sparta from that given by Herodotus this is not due only to the subject and method of the two authors. The fifty years following the Persian wars had been a period of almost constant friction between the two powers, culminating in thirty years of war which as it went on drew in all Greece on one side or the other and left both sides exhausted and embittered. Attitudes were polarized as never before. Sparta and Athens, oligarchy and democracy, Dorian and Ionian, were presented as stark antitheses, first in the propaganda and finally in the everyday thinking of both sides. This polarization is reflected in Thucydides, especially in the speeches in which he reports current arguments, but also in his narrative, as when he records the incredulity with which the Spartan surrender at Sphacteria was received in Greece.

Though he spent twenty years in exile and so could draw information from both sides, Thucydides found the Spartans uncommunicative and seems to have relied mainly on their allies for his material, so that though he tells us the results of Spartan policy he has little to say of its motives or of how it was decided. Only two Spartans, Archidamus and Brasidas, come through as individuals, compared to the many lively portraits of Athenians. Archidamus, born before Thermopylae and already king in 464, is the pattern of cautious conservatism. 'Sagacious and moderate', he is the spokesman for the peace party in the debate before the war, urging the Spartans to vote if not for peace at least for a diplomatic delay to allow for adequate preparation. Outvoted, he led the annual invasion of Attica until his death. In the aristocratic tradition, his interests beyond Sparta included ties of hospitality with Pericles. Brasidas was a pure soldier, a dashing young officer who could turn defeat into victory. He had also an unusual gift for diplomacy and was, Thucydides says, not a bad speaker – for a Spartan. Breaking away from the cautious strategy of Archidamus, he carried the war into the heart of the Athenian empire at the head of a force of enfranchised helots, and at the time of his death was considered the leader of the war party.

In contrast to these two, each of whom in his way represents the Spartan virtues, was the regent Pausanias, whom Thucydides pairs with Themistocles and whose later career he describes in an unusually long digression in his introductory book. Sent out after the withdrawal of Leotychidas to command the Greeks in the Aegean, he repelled them by his arrogance and was recalled to Sparta and acquitted of a charge of medism. Returning to Byzantium as a private individual, he lived in Persian style and sought Xerxes's daughter in marriage, hoping thereby to become tyrant of all Greece. Recalled again, he was arrested by the ephors and charged with conspiring with the helots to overthrow the state. He fled to the temple of Athena on the acropolis and was besieged there till on the point of death by starvation, being dragged out just in time to avoid polluting the temple by dying in it. Such was the end of the victor of Plataea, at least in the official version which Thucydides evidently followed.

Thucydides tells us little directly of Spartan institutions, which he believed had remained unchanged for more than eight hundred years counting from the end of the war.[17] He does, however, in his account of the debates leading to the declaration of war, give a full and clear account of the way in which the policy of the Spartan alliance was determined. The question of war with Athens was first debated in the Spartan assembly, where Archidamus spoke against the single ephor who was in favour of it. The same ephor then put it to the vote and it was carried, not in this case by acclamation but, exceptionally, by a division. Representatives of the allies were allowed to address the assembly, but not to vote. After this, the question was put to a specially convened congress of the allies, and being carried by them became the policy of 'the Lacedaemonians and their allies'. The same procedure was followed to adopt the Peace of Nicias in 421, but then four of the allies voted against an alliance and refused to be bound by it, so that it had to be supplemented by a treaty between the Spartans alone and the Athenians.[18]

The number of Spartiates had shrunk appreciably since Plataea, partly because of the earthquake of 464 which had almost wiped out the city and partly because of continuing war casualties, notably at Sphacteria. Helots were used as hoplites, perhaps for the first time, in Brasidas's expedition to Thrace, and later they formed an appreciable element in armies serving overseas, as well as presumably furnishing light troops. When, Thucydides says, the Spartans invited those who claimed to have served with distinction to come forward and be rewarded with their freedom, more than two thousand did so. Soon afterwards they all disappeared and 'no man knew how each one had been killed'. Such was the fear now inspired by their numbers and discontent. Later Thucydides speaks of the Spartans taking the field against Argos, 'themselves and the helots, in full force'.[19]

Seldom very interested in the details of military organization, Thucydides gives in his fifth book an exceptionally detailed account of the battle of Mantinea, fought in 418 by the Spartans and Tegeans against the Mantineans, Argives and Athenians, including a description of the Spartan order of battle which he used to calculate their number. But the account raises a number of difficulties. This book did not receive its final revision, and it seems likely that here, as elsewhere in it, we have notes from different sources which, had the author lived, would have been combined into a single more concise narrative. In its present form, there is what seems to be a description of the battle taken from a participant hostile to king Agis and ignorant of his tactics, followed by a later note from some source on the formation of the Spartan army, with some errors for which either Thucydides or his informant may be responsible. In the first part the Spartan chain of command, which gave the Spartan army a flexibility unique among hoplite armies of the time, is stressed. In the second the units through which this chain operated are set out as a means of calculating the numbers engaged.

Taking the latter with a somewhat similar description by Xenophon of the organization of the Spartan army some twenty-five years later, we see that there had been a change between the battles of Plataea and Mantinea, perhaps as a result of the earthquake and Messenian revolt of 464. Instead of regiments based, at least nominally, on the residential quarters of the city which had replaced the primitive tribes with the coming of the hoplite army and had still been in use at Plataea, we now have purely military units, which could incorporate *perioeci* as well as Spartans. The largest unit was the brigade (*mora*), of which there were six, each commanded by a *polemarch* taking his orders direct from the king. Each brigade consisted of two or four regiments (*lochoi*) – Thucydides seems to confuse these two terms – each regiment of two companies (*pentekonteres*), and each company of two platoons (*enomotiae*). The numbers in each unit depended on the number of age-groups called up, but the platoon seems to have contained, if at full strength, about thirty-two men. Each unit had its own officer through whom the orders of the *polemarch* were passed down and each could at need function independently should it become detached.

The system was impressive, but not infallible. At Mantinea, as at Plataea, the king's plan was nearly wrecked by the disobedience of one of the officers, perhaps politically motivated. The Spartans are said to have been taken by surprise, coming while still in marching order upon their opponents drawn up for battle. The day was saved by the steadiness of the rank and file against the headlong charge of their opponents, and their victory was due not to professional skill or training, but solely to their courage.[20]

11
Later Writers

From the peak of 404 the decline of Sparta was swift and irretrievable. Hailed everywhere as the liberators of Greece, her officers soon proved more cynical and more corrupt than the Athenians had ever been. A second Athenian empire grew up on a more liberal basis, and on land a new combination emerged, headed by Thebes. In 371 the Theban general Epaminondas defeated the army of Sparta and her allies at Leuctra. Of seven hundred Spartiates – five-sixths of all those of military age – who fought in the battle, four hundred were killed. In the next year Laconia was invaded, for the first time since the arrival of the Dorians, and an enemy army camped on the outskirts of Sparta. The restoration of Messenian independence in 369, after more than three hundred years of Spartan domination, dealt a shrewd blow to the Spartiate economy, and the establishment of Megalopolis as the capital of an Arcadian federation and a stronghold blocking the north-western route from Laconia ensured that Sparta would from now on be a second-rate power.

At the same time the old way of life, now increasingly identified with 'Lycurgus', was undermined. As a result of the wars in Asia Minor and the Hellespont, gold and silver coinage had flooded into the country in spite of legislation to stem the tide, and relaxation of the traditional restrictions on the alienation of land accentuated the growing inequality of wealth. Economic pressures combined with the long-term demographic effects of the great earthquake of 464 and the casualties of battle to reduce drastically the numbers of full Spartiates, so that Spartan armies depended more and more, especially for foreign service, on enfranchised helots and mercenaries, with no more than a stiffening of Spartan officers. How isolated the diminished number of Spartiates had become was dramatically shown in 397 by the conspiracy, abortive though it was, of Cinadon, one of the new class of 'inferiors' or Spartans without the means to pay their mess dues.

Xenophon witnessed the whole of this process. A young man when Athens fell, he soon afterwards joined the Greek army raised by Cyrus for his revolt against the Great King, and was one of the leaders of the Ten Thousand in their adventurous march to the Black Sea. He served under several Spartan generals around the Hellespont and became friendly with King Agesilaus, with whom he returned to Greece in 394. Exiled by Athens, he was given by Sparta a country property at Scillus, near Olympia, where he lived until he was driven out following the battle of Leuctra; after which he lived at Corinth and finally, his exile having been rescinded, at Athens. In his *Hellenica* or Greek History, he first completed Thucydides's history to the fall of Athens, and later narrated in a prosaic and factual style with a minimum of comment the military and political events of the years down to the death of Epaminondas in battle at Mantinea in 362. Writing first at Scillus and then at Corinth he relied on personal knowledge and hearsay, and his focus is Peloponnesian rather than Spartan, except where Agesilaus is involved. The later books show progressive disillusion with Sparta and attraction to the glamorous figure of Epaminondas.

Much more influential in forming the later picture of Sparta was an early work, written soon after his return to Greece from Asia. This little pamphlet, generally known as the *Constitution of the Lacedaemonians*, makes no pretence to be either history or sociology, but is a piece of special pleading designed to reconcile the Greeks to Spartan supremacy by showing that it is inevitable, and perhaps a little to justify to himself his own defection from Athens. The pamphlet gives a very simplified and tendentious account of Spartan social, educational and military practices, all ascribed indiscriminately to Lycurgus, designed to show that they are exclusively directed to military ends. There is no sign of research or even of personal observation. Xenophon may have picked up some of his ideas from the expatriate Spartans in Asia, and some from the entourage of Agesilaus, whose policy was to encourage a return to the old ways against the prevailing corruption. The rest is pure fiction. Thus Xenophon, the last writer to have known Sparta while the old ways still had some life, is one of the first exponents of the myth. Henceforth the myth prevails, and the more the glories of Sparta receded the greater the tendency to romanticize her institutions.

The most important writer of the next generation was Aristotle. In his anatomy of the Greek city-state, the *Politics*, he makes only passing references to Spartan history, but is critical of Spartan institutions and paints a vivid picture of the complete breakdown of Spartan society in his own time – a dwindling citizen body, extreme inequality of property with two-fifths of the land owned by women, and prevailing greed and luxury.[1] Of the preliminary study of Sparta, one of the 158 sketches of the constitutional histories of Greek cities compiled in preparation for his major work, unfortunately only insignificant fragments have survived, though it was used by Plutarch and others.

Ephorus, an older contemporary of Aristotle, wrote among other things a general history of Greece from the return of the Heraclids to his own time in thirty books which remained throughout antiquity the standard work on the period it covered, but which is known to us only so far as it was quoted or followed by later writers. A pupil of the Athenian orator and publicist Isocrates, he was a 'literary' historian – he also wrote a book on style – whose main concern was to produce a connected and attractive synthesis from his wide but uncritical reading. He was probably responsible for combining the various and sometimes conflicting legends about Lycurgus into a consecutive biography and presenting him as a historical person. One passage preserved by Strabo gives an account of the Dorian occupation of Laconia and the origin of the helots which is different from that generally accepted later, and more consistent with the archaeological evidence. According to this, the Dorians took possession of a land most of whose inhabitants had emigrated to Ionia or the northern Peloponnese. The kings, Eurysthenes and Proclus, divided the country into six parts. They kept Sparta for themselves and allotted Amyclae as a reward to the man who had betrayed it to them; for the rest, they built townships and sent out 'kings' to rule them, accepting as settlers anyone who chose to come and having equal rights with the Spartans. In the next generation, however, Agis, the son of Eurysthenes, sought to subordinate the outlying parts to Sparta; most accepted this, but the people of the plain of Helos resisted, and were converted into public slaves with fixed domicile and obligations.[2]

Of writers later than the fourth century little need be said. The last who seems to have added anything new was Sosibius, himself a native Lacedaemonian, who worked at Alexandria about the beginning of the third century. Fragments surviving from his work on Lacedaemonian religious ceremonies are interesting, since such ceremonies often preserve the memory of events associated with them long after they would otherwise have been forgotten. In the second half of the third century the attempted social revolution of Cleomenes III purporting to restore a now highly theoretical 'Lycurgan' constitution gave rise to a new burst of pamphleteering, strongly coloured by Stoic philosophy, which had some influence on Plutarch.

Plutarch's *Parallel Lives*, written at the beginning of the second century AD, are biographical essays, primarily moral in purpose. Based on wide if not critical reading, his life of Lycurgus, and to a less extent those of Lysander, Agesilaus, Agis, Cleomenes and the Athenian Cimon, give a conspectus of the literary material, good, bad and indifferent, available in his day. Because of his readability, and the lack of other sources, the life of Lycurgus has, along with Xenophon, been the principal channel for the transmission of the Spartan myth to this day.

Half a century later, Pausanias in his *Guide to Greece* performed for the material remains extant in his time a service somewhat similar to that of Plutarch for the literary sources. Travelling systematically through Greece he describes the main points of interest, the topography, buildings, statues and monuments that he saw and tells us whatever he could discover about their history and the traditions associated with them. He seems to have been an honest recorder, and his accounts of Laconia and Olympia provide a useful supplement to the surviving archaeological record, though one that must be used with some caution. On the other hand his detailed story of the Messenian wars, drawn from Alexandrian epic poetry, is historically worthless.

It remains to consider certain documents, not strictly literary, which are found only in later writers but may have an earlier base. The first type consists of lists of kings, ephors and victors at religious festivals, which were later used to establish a chronological framework. Lists of the kings of both royal houses, the Agiad and the Eurypontid, going back to the twin sons of Aristomenes, who led the Dorians into Laconia, are already found in Herodotus in a form not very different from that which later became standard. Such lists were likely to have been transmitted orally over a long period, since they were easily memorized and were in a sense the title-deeds of the reigning monarch. The list of the Agiads may well be substantially correct, that of the junior line of Eurypontids contains in its early part some suspiciously allegorical names, and was perhaps padded to bring it into line with the other.

The first king known independently of the lists is Theopompus, the victor of the first Messenian war in the eighth century. From Leon and Agasicles in the early sixth century we have a continuous record outside the lists and at least approximate dates, while from Cleomenes and Demaratus at the end of that century links with known events become more frequent and dates correspondingly more accurate. It is important to note that the original lists were simply of successive reigns, not genealogies in the strict sense, so that it was possible to attach Lycurgus to either family. Dates were assigned to the reigns in the late fifth or fourth century, when they were calculated by giving an arbitrary length to a generation and assuming that each king came from a new generation. The allocation of events to the earlier reigns came later still, and was a product of the Hellenistic historical imagination.

The list of ephors is later. It was unknown to Herodotus, who refers to the ephors collectively and without names, and to Chilon simply as 'a Spartan of repute' and 'the wisest of the Spartans', not as ephor. When in the sixth century Sparta was brought into closer contact with other states some less clumsy and more exact form of dating than that by kings was needed, and the recognition of one ephor to give his name to the year was perhaps copied from the Athenian use of the eponymous archon. Our first example of this system, which implies not only the distinction of one ephor from his colleagues, but the existence of a recognized and accessible list, is the inscription of Damonon. In Thucydides it is used in the official texts of the Peace of Nicias in 421 and the treaty with Persia in 411; also in the passage in which he sets out to fix exactly the year of the beginning of the Peloponnesian War with a triple reference to the Spartan ephor, the Athenian archon and the Argive priestess of Hera.[3] Later writers attributed the creation of the ephorate to Lycurgus or to Theopompus, but Sosibius seems to have made Chilon, in the middle of the sixth century, the first ephor. Since the office is also found at Thera and in a colony of Tarentum, it was probably an early Dorian office the powers and functions of which were extended from time to time. A list going back to 754 (wrongly thought to fall in the reign of Theopompus) was certainly fictitious, but an authentic list may have gone back to 556, the year given for Chilon.

A list of winners of the foot race at the Olympic games, from 776, the supposed date of their establishment, was drawn up in the fifth century by Hippias of Elis, probably from lists or dedications preserved in the temple of Zeus, and a much later version of this list has been preserved. Its use as a framework for a general chronology transcending local systems dates from the Hellenistic period. It can be supplemented for other events from inscriptions and other sources, and though there are some reservations about the earlier names, the list looks authentic and is probably in general reliable.

The extended list of winners shows an interesting pattern. At first the winners all came from Elis and Messenia, with the latter predominating. The last Messenian victory was in 736, at the eleventh games, and after this the north-eastern Peloponnese begins to appear. At the fifteenth Olympiad (720) a Spartan won the long-distance race, and from the sixteenth to the fifty-seventh (716–552) Spartan or Laconian winners are frequent, with 22 wins recorded in the foot race and 16 in other events. After this athletic victories by Spartans are rare, and no Spartan won the foot race until 316; but from about the end of the sixth century to 392 nine victories in the four-horse chariot race are known, beginning with that of king Demaratus and ending with Kyniska, sister of king Agesilaus, the first woman, according to Pausanias, to own race-horses and to win at Olympia. Pausanias says that her example was followed by other Spartan women, but the only one we know won in 368 with a two-horse chariot.

A list of winners at the musical competitions at the Spartan festival of Carnean Apollo was compiled in the fifth century by Hellanicus of Lesbos, perhaps based on temple records but more probably on family traditions, since the only names he is known to have recorded are those of non-Spartans; his list began with his countryman Terpander, and Sosibius equated the date of the festival's foundation with the twenty-sixth Olympiad (676–672).

The writers of the fourth century and later had no body of written records on which to draw for Sparta as they had for Athens. Even there, as Jacoby has shown, these hardly reached farther back than the fifth century, and Aristotle could be taken in by forgeries of the 'ancient constitution' circulated at the end of that century. It is sometimes claimed that the Spartan 'government', or at least the ephors, must have kept archives, but there is no evidence for this, and all we know of Spartan methods makes it unlikely except in the case of treaties with other states, which must have been put in writing and preserved, perhaps in the form of inscriptions set up on the borders. It is likely, too, that the kings preserved oracles given in response to official enquiries. Of other public records there is no trace, a fact later explained by a 'rhetra' of Lycurgus which forbade his laws to be written down. The uniqueness of the 'Great Rhetra' preserved by Plutarch,[4] who probably took it from Aristotle and who believed it to be an oracle given to Lycurgus to confirm his establishment of the council of elders, with a later postscript added by Theopompus, makes this document, which has called forth so much scholarship and ingenuity, suspect. The extraordinary archaic language, sometimes adduced as evidence of its genuineness, seems more like that of an antiquarian forger seeking to give his work a spurious air of authenticity, while where the content differs from the oracle paraphrased by Tyrtaeus it seems less consistent with the constitutional practice described by Thucydides and Xenophon. If genuine, as most modern scholars have assumed, the 'rhetra' will form part of the settlement between gentry and hoplites after the second Messenian war also described by Tyrtaeus, but it is more likely that it is a forgery of king Pausanias or his circle in the early fourth century.

12
Conclusions

When in the ninth century the Dorians, part of the last wave of Greek-speaking migrants to enter the peninsula, reached Laconia they found only a sparse and scattered population with no organized centres. Coming down from the north-west they settled first in the fertile plain of Sparta, and their leaders divided this and the surrounding foothills among themselves. Lesser folk and late comers pushed out into the poorer country between Parnon and Taygetus, establishing townships to manage their local affairs, but remaining part of the people who came to be called 'the Lacedaemonians'. These were the outdwellers or *perioeci*. They had some degree of autonomy because of their distance from the central government, their relation to which, at first undefined, perhaps later gave rise to some conflict of which an echo is preserved by Ephorus. Because of the lack of population any previous inhabitants, as well as volunteers from outside, were absorbed into the Dorian community. The process of settlement, which occupied something like a century, was peaceful, except perhaps for some skirmishes around shrines like Amyclae; there were no successive conquests such as those imagined by Hellenistic scholars to flesh out the bare lists of kings, and no marked racial or cultural differences.

So much we can infer from the archaeological remains. The historical record proper begins with the conquest of the upper Messenian plain in the third quarter of the eighth century, when the settlement of Laconia was complete, economic security had been attained and external trade was beginning. The war, which lasted twenty years, had been one of the heroic type, and the chief beneficiaries were the nobles of the plain, who annexed the conquered land and reduced its inhabitants to tenants paying half their produce to their new lords.

Two generations or so later, possibly after a defeat of Sparta by Argos on her northern frontier, the Messenians revolted. They were supported by those of their countrymen who had not been conquered in the first war and by some of their Arcadian neighbours. It took the Spartans nearly twenty years to gain the upper hand; then they did so only because they adopted the new method of hoplite warfare, which called for a trained and disciplined force of armoured spearmen. Lacking the prosperous farmers from whom such armies were usually drawn, Sparta had to create a hoplite class artificially by assigning allotments of land and providing the necessary labour for their cultivation during the absence on service of their owners. The land will have come from public land or land acquired from *perioeci*, not from the estates of the aristocracy, and the men would be recruited from the retainers of the nobles and from other volunteers. By the end of the war foreign service had welded the hoplites into a coherent group with common interests and a strong *esprit de corps*, and subsequently they were able, after a struggle, to keep their allotments and to participate on the same terms in the division of the Messenian lands, with their conquered inhabitants as tied cultivators. Their position was reinforced by a constitutional settlement giving them, perhaps with the help of the kings, a defined place in the state at the expense of the nobles.

This system depended on the helots who cultivated the allotments. They could not leave the land and had to pay a fixed amount in kind to its holder, keeping any surplus for themselves. They were not, however, the property of the landholder, who could not sell, evict or maltreat them. The government, not the master, was responsible for their discipline and could call upon them for service as light-armed troops. The fixed contribution was calculated to be sufficient to pay the mess dues of the holder of the allotment and support his family, but not to allow him to enrich himself.

The origin of the helots is uncertain. The theory commonly held in later antiquity and in modern times, that they represented the pre-Dorian population enslaved by conquest, cannot be reconciled with the archaeological evidence and is not found before the historian Theopompus in the late fourth century. Herodotus takes the helots, as the lowest class of Spartan society, for granted. His contemporary, Antiochus of Syracuse, says that Lacedaemonians (i.e. *perioeci*) who refused to take part in the first Messenian war 'were enslaved and called helots'; Ephorus, in the fourth century, that the first helots were *perioeci* who, in the second generation of the settlement, resisted the central control of Sparta. Either way, they differed from the *perioeci* only in status, not in race. Their importance and definition, if not their origin, dates from the creation of a hoplite class in the second Messenian war, and they were probably drawn from the landless labourers and poor tenant-farmers found in every archaic Greek society. After the war the same status was extended to the Messenians whose lands were annexed, but these remained a distinct group, retaining a strong sense of national identity and always prone, unlike the Laconian helots, to rebellion. All the recorded 'helot revolts' were actually Messenian revolts, national, not social, in origin. Revolts of Laconian helots existed only in the nightmares of the hoplite class, and sometimes in its propaganda.

From the second Messenian war to the end of the fifth century, there were two classes of Spartan citizens with very different ways of life, values and attitudes, tensions between which explain much Spartan history. On one side were the old landed gentry, established, competitive and cosmopolitan; on the other the new rank-and-file hoplites, defensive, egalitarian and conformist. In the creation and establishment of this second class, if anywhere, lay the 'Spartan revolution', but its results did not appear at once. The hoplites were at first content to follow the lead of the gentry in taste as in politics, while they grew accustomed to their status and to the solidarity fostered by the common meals. The immediate sequel to the Messenian war was not austerity but a new wave of luxury and artistic achievement, seen in the poems of Alcman and in the exhuberance of Laconian II artefacts in ivory and bronze. The succession of Olympic victories continued. Foreign contacts grew wider, and the export of pottery and of decorated bronze vessels began.

The war with Tegea began early in the sixth century as a war for arable land. It was ended, about the middle of the century, by the adoption of a new policy which aimed not at conquest but at the creation of a buffer zone of allied states between Sparta and the outside world. Argos stood out, but her defeat at Thyrea in 546 secured the northern frontier for a generation and the absorption of Cynuria and Cythera warded off seaborne invasion. The new policy, sometimes associated with Chilon who was ephor in 556, was essentially defensive and reflected the interests of the hoplites, who had most to lose and least to gain from foreign adventures. The growing ascendancy of hoplite values is also seen in the absence after 552 of Spartan names from the list of winners of the foot race at Olympia.

The war with Tegea did not interfere with art and trade. Laconian III pottery and the great bronze bowls were exported more widely than ever, and gold was sought from Lydia for a statue of Apollo. Links were especially close with Samos and Corinth, and they may have provided the carriers for much of the trade. After the middle of the century external trade declined, not because of any change in Sparta, but because of the Mediterranean-wide competition of Athens and of upheavals in the barbarian world of Persians, Carhaginians and Celts. Thrown back onto the local market, Spartan artists turned from vase painting and the casting of large bronze vessels to increased production of sculpture in stone and of small bronze figures. There is no falling off in quality, and sculpture especially was stimulated by the employment of an Ionian artist, Bathycles of Magnesia, to adorn a throne for Apollo at Amyclae. About the same time another foreigner, Theodorus of Samos, a famous architect and metal worker who had worked for Croesus and Polycrates, built the Shade House, an assemby hall near the market, and a local artist, Gitiadas, was decorating a splendid new temple for Athena on the acropolis, the Bronze House. A wider public than before is perhaps suggested by the popularity of the 'hero reliefs' to adorn local shrines in various parts of Laconia and in the realistic figures of hoplites which now make their appearance side by side with the aristocratic girls of the mirror handles.

For all the headstrong brilliance that Herodotus ascribes to him, Cleomenes continued the hoplite foreign policy, seeking to extend the defensive ring of allies and contain Argos, while shunning adventures overseas. The opposite party is represented by his half-brother Dorieus who, rather than accept a subordinate place, went off with his friends to seek a fortune in the west, and by his rival Demaratus with his chariot racing, foreign connections and ability to adapt himself to exile at the Persian court.

It was Thermopylae that finally imposed the hoplite image on Sparta, giving reality to the myth and projecting it to the rest of Greece, where it was henceforth skilfully exploited by Spartan diplomacy. At home what had been the propaganda of a party became the ideology of the state, rigidly enforced and eventually universally believed. The process was strengthened by the long rivalry with Athens, culminating in the Peloponnesian War. The regent Pausanias, with his Coan guest-friend, his grand manners and his unbounded ambition was the last of the old aristocrats, and he was destroyed; the charges against him, arrogance, intrigue with Persia and plotting a helot revolt, are significant.

The years immediately after the Persian wars saw too the last products of a distinctive Laconian art and the last burst of important public buildings, the war-memorial colonnade in the market-place with its columns in the form of statues of the Persian leaders, and the rebuilding and enlargement of the Menelaeum.[1] The latter, with its massive terrace of squared stone rising 8 m (26 ft) above the top of the bluff on which it stood and with its parapet of blue limestone and marble, looked across the river to Taygetus, dominating the valley below. With Athena's Bronze House to the north and the lofty 'throne' and statue of Apollo to the south, it completed a semicircle of striking shrines that crowned the rim of the hollow in which Sparta was built, visible alike from anywhere in the city and from afar on its approaches.

In his guide book Pausanias tells us, from the evidence of the dedications at Olympia, that after the Persian wars the Spartans took up horse breeding with more enthusiasm than any other Greeks,[2] and we know the names of some ten Spartan winners of the Olympic chariot race between 468 and 368, as well as a few, like Demaratus, earlier. In fact the gentry, effectively excluded from public life, turned to sport, in the form which best allowed the competitive display of wealth and skill not only against one another but among their peers from the rest of Greece gathered at the great pan-Hellenic festivals. Thus the gentry survived, though with greatly diminished influence. Archidamus, the friend of Pericles, and Brasidas with his way with non-Spartans and his wide strategic horizons displayed, in their different ways, some of the gentry qualities, but Archidamus was overruled by the assembly on the vital question of war with Athens in 434 and Brasidas was killed in Thrace commanding an inadequate force of enfranchised helots. More typical was the wealthy Lichas, whose chariot won at Olympia in 420; he represented Argos at Sparta and later served as one of eleven commissioners with the admiral in Asia, where his protest against Persian territorial claims caused Tissaphernes to break off negotiations with Sparta.

But though the hoplites ruled Sparta they could not win the war with Athens. For this, the collaboration of Persia and funds to maintain mercenary fleets and armies were needed. The subtle and ingratiating Lysander with his obscure birth and unscrupulous ambition represented a new kind of threat to the 'Spartan way of life', as did the influx of wealth and corruption unleashed by his conquests. The unsuccessful attempt to ban the possession of gold and silver coin, naturally attributed to Lycurgus, belongs to this period.[3] Traditional restrictions on the alienation of allotments were relaxed and land accumulated in a few hands, filling the city with 'inferiors', Spartan by birth but without the privileges of citizens. Agesilaus tried in vain to turn back the tide, even encouraging his sister to enter chariots at Olympia to show that this needed only money, not any manly qualities; he died abroad as a leader of mercenaries in an attempt to replenish Sparta's exchequer. After Leuctra, apart from the short-lived attempt of Agis and Cleomenes in the third century to restore a doctrinaire Stoic version of the 'Lycurgan' state, Sparta declined to the position of a comfortable provincial town, cherishing the myth of its past in proportion to its irrelevance to the present, and finally reviving and brutalizing it as an attraction for Roman tourists.

Almost all Spartan institutions, political and social, were at some time ascribed to Lycurgus, of whom Plutarch wrote in the second century AD:

> 'Of the lawgiver Lycurgus absolutely nothing can be said that is not controversial, either about his birth, his travels or his death. Every writer gives a different version of his laws and social system. Least of all is there any agreement as to his date.'[24]

We are no wiser now, and it is well to admit that there is no good evidence for Lycurgus as a real person; he is a product of the Greek propensity to explain history in personal terms. He was unknown to or ignored by Tyrtaeus, Pindar and Hellanicus, and in our earliest account Herodotus uses the style of myth rather than history. Almost as an afterthought, he made him the uncle of the fourth Agiad king, but this was a guess, and most later writers follow Simonides in making his nephew a Eurypontid two generations later. He was probably a primitive demigod with a shrine by the Eurotas, who was adopted by the hoplites some time after the Messenian war and invoked by their leaders to give a respectable cloak of antiquity to new applications of custom or new regulations, so that he became a symbol of hoplite values. For Xenophon he was already an abstract model of the wise lawgiver, while Ephorus gave him a human face by blending the various legends into biographical form.

Outwardly conservative, retaining the structure of the heroic age and avoiding the revolutions which disrupted most Greek states in the Archaic period, the constitution of Sparta was in fact evolving to meet changing circumstances. The existence side by side of two royal families helped the survival of the monarchy by halving the risk of incapacity and by providing in the tendency for the kings to take opposite sides a safety valve for controversy without involving the institution itself. As 'kings of the Lacedaemonians', they commanded the loyalty of the *perioeci* and were a force for unity. By the sixth century they had lost all their domestic powers, retaining only ceremonial and religious functions along with great prestige and wealth. They remained supreme commanders of the army in the field, though the right to make war on any state they wished was not exercised after the fiasco of Cleomenes's invasion of Attica in 506. After this, too, it was forbidden for both kings to take the field together, the choice being apparently made on each occasion by the assembly. The power to end a campaign, inherent in the supreme command, was curbed in the fifth century following accusations of bribery, by attaching two ephors to the army to oversee diplomatic negotiations.

In the sixth and fifth centuries all major decisions of policy, at least in the field of foreign relations on which alone we have information, were made by the full citizen assembly. Though limited to hoplites belonging to a mess, this was still as large as many democratic assemblies and, like them, could be swayed by appeals to emotion or superstition. This assembly is referred to by Herodotus sometimes as 'the Spartiates' but more commonly as 'the Lacedaemonians' and its decisions were binding on the *perioeci*, though they were not represented. Decisions involving the allies, on the other hand, were first made by the Spartan assembly and then referred to a special convention of the allies for confirmation or rejection. Naturally, foreign envoys would seek the support of some influential person, a king or, later, the ephors, before approaching the assembly for its decision.

The council, originally consisting of the heads of the noble families, had not gained the powers of an oligarchy but rather its power had declined in line with that of the kings. At some time, perhaps after the second Messenian war, membership had been made elective and limited to twenty-eight, together with the kings, one of whom presided. Members were now chosen by the assembly by acclamation from citizens over the age of sixty and held office for life. Aristotle in his schematic account of the Spartan constitution of his day makes them represent the gentry and says that election was coveted as a reward of 'excellence'; it is likely that, by custom rather than by law, candidates were usually drawn from the old families of the plain. By the sixth century the council had lost most of its powers, though it was still the court for certain crimes, notably for charges of misconduct against a king. It did not, as Aristotle wrongly claims, have a monopoly of preparing business for the assembly, but sometimes no doubt it discussed such business and the views of its members, who had first right to speak, would carry much weight.

A later and distinctive element in the Spartan state was the board of five ephors, elected annually from the whole citizen body and holding office for one year only. The title was an old one, being found in some other Dorian cities traditionally associated with Sparta, but the importance of the office dates from the middle of the sixth century and continued to grow throughout the fifth. The original functions of the ephors seem to have concerned the maintenance of public order and, by extension, the succession in the royal families, and it is thus that they appear in the sixth century in Herodotus. Their small number and the fact that they were continuously in session made them suitable agents for actions requiring speed and secrecy, and their representative character and annual election would enable them to anticipate the likely reaction of the assembly, but their duties were always executive, not deliberative. When the assembly had decided on war and named the commander it fell to the ephors to call up the army and decide its strength, and so probably Pheidippides in 490 and certainly the Athenian envoys in 479 addressed themselves to the ephors, not the assembly. In the fourth century the ephors served as the channel for instructions to generals serving abroad. Occasionally individual ephors like Sthenelaides in 433/2 played a political role, and by this time one of them acted as chairman of the assembly. The use of one ephor to give his name to the year is first found in the fifth century in the inscription of Damonon, and later in official documents like the Peace of Nicias in 421 and in the elaborate cross-dating by which Thucydides fixes the beginning of the Peloponnesian War. In Herodotus the ephors are always referred to collectively and anonymously, and Chilon is indentified only as 'the wisest of the Spartans', not as an ephor.

We come at last to the famous *agoge*, the rigid system which is supposed to have controlled in every detail the life of the Spartan male from seven to sixty and even beyond. The roots of this lie deep in the primitive history of the Dorian tribes long before they reached Laconia. That the customs on which it was based survived more clearly in Sparta, and to some extent in Crete, than elsewhere in Greece may be ascribed to the late migration of the Dorians from their northern homeland, and to the fact that those that came to Sparta had little or no contact with the sub-Mycenaean culture either on their route south or in Laconia itself, as well as to the isolation of the latter during the period of settlement. It would be natural for these customs to be preserved to some extent among the aristocracy and not among the out-settlers of the frontier.

In its later fully developed form the Spartan system was clearly, like the constitution, the result not of a single act of legislation but of a long process of evolution. Unfortunately this process is hidden from us. Though both Alcman and Herodotus refer incidentally to the common mess, without any indication of its central position in Spartan life, our earliest account in any detail is that of Xenophon, partial and for many reasons unreliable, and we owe most of our information to much later authors, notably Plutarch.

All the evidence suggests that until the fifth century most Spartans lived very much like other Greeks, in a society which was somewhat rustic compared to those of Athens or Corinth, but with its own active cultural tradition. As in all Greek communities there were a number of local peculiarities, of which the most important were the survival of certain primitive customs and, after the second Messenian war, the existence of an artificially created *rentier* class of citizens, divorced both from direct contact with the soil and from large-scale economic activity. Another peculiarity which later gave rise to scandal in the rest of Greece was the freedom and independence allowed to women, partly a legacy of the aristocratic tradition, partly a product of the club-centred life of the men. The archaeological finds presuppose a considerable degree of trade, internal as well as export, but this did not require coinage, for it could have been carried on by barter. Since iron was one Laconian product in wide demand, the famous iron 'spits' may have been a rudimentary unit of account, though not a substitute for currency. In addition to iron and lead, Laconia produced abundance of wool and woollen cloth, leather and skins and the famous crimson dye, all of which would have been available for export. For geographical reasons most of this trade would have been carried on by *perioeci*, nor is it likely that the Spartan gentry were more commercially minded than aristocrats elsewhere. Ordinary craftsmen, potters, smiths and fashioners of cheap images in clay and lead were common and wide-spread. Those of a better class, capable of producing work of artistic quality, were never numerous, and were probably concentrated in or near Sparta, where their basic market was. They catered primarily for the gentry, but the host of cheap imitations show that the tastes of the gentry were followed, within their economic limits, by all classes, and they were shared too by the well-to-do *perioeci* of central and southern Laconia. Though few in number, the artists were sufficiently numerous to develop and maintain a strong local style, whatever the material, which was doubtless transmitted from father to son or master to apprentice, to be modified in each generation by contact with the the work of outside artists, whether gained from imports, by travel, or at festivals like that at Olympia. Not until the fifth century, when the rest of Greece entered the age of the individual and often peripatetic artist, did the local craftsmen of Laconia sink, with few exceptions, to the commonplace and derivative.

Chronological Table 1 Archaeology

BC	*Sparta*	*Peloponnese*	*Athens*	*East Greece and Islands*
900		Protogeometric (Corinth & Argos)	Protogeometric	
850	Protogeometric	Early Geometric (Corinth & Argos)	Early Geometric	
800		Middle Geometric (Corinth & Argos)	Middle Geometric	Geometric
750	Geometric	Late Geometric Argos 750–700 Corinth 750–725 Early Protocorinthian 725–700	Late Geometric 750–710 Early Protoattic 710–680	
700	First Temple of Orthia 'Lady of the Menelaeum' Early ivories	Middle Protocorinthian	Middle Protoattic	'Bird bowls' 700–600 'Wild Goat' style 675–575
650	Laconian I Daedalic	Late Protocorinthian	Late Protoattic 650–610	'Nicandre' statue 650 'Lady of Auxerre' 630
625	Laconian II 'Post Daedalic'	Early Corinthian	'Apollo' from Sunium 615 Early Black Figure 610–550	
600		Temple of Hera at Olympia 600 Middle Corinthian Statues of Cleobis and Biton (Argos) 600–580		Seated figures at Didyma 600–550
575	Temple of Orthia rebuilt 580 Laconian III Early Archaic	Late Corinthian 'Apollo' of Tenea	Middle Black Figure 570–525	'Fikellura 575–500 Temple of Hera at Samos 560
550	Laconian IV Middle Archaic 'Bronze House' of Athena 'Throne of Apollo' at Amyclaeum	Temple of Apollo at Corinth 540	Late Black Figure 530–450 'Peplos Maiden' from Acropolis 530 Early Red Figure 530–500 Gravestone of Aristion 510	Temple of Artemis at Ephesus 530
500	Laconian V Late Archaic 'Leonidas' statue Menelaeum 'Persian Colonnade'		Late Archaic Red Figure	Temple of Aphaea at Aegina
475	Early Classical	Charioteer at Delphi Temple of Zeus at Olympia 460	Classical Red Figure	
450		Temple of Apollo at Bassae 450–425	Parthenon 447–433	

Chronological Table 2 Traditional History

BC	*Kings of Sparta* Agiad	Eurypontid	*Spartan History*	*External Events*
900	Agis I 930–900		Foundation of Sparta 1000	
	Echestratus 900–870	Eurypon 895–865		
850	Leobotas 870–840	Prytanis 865–835		
	Dorrusas 840–815	Polydectes 830–805	Reforms of Lycurgus 800	
	Agesilaus I 815–785	Eunomus 805–775		First Olympiad 775 'Homer'
750	Archilaus 785–760	Charillus 775–750	Ephor List begins 754	Trade with west begins
	Telechus 760–740	Nicandrus 750–720	Siege of Amyclae 750–740	Syracuse and Corcyra founded 734
			Capture of Helos 740	
	Alcamenus I 740–700		First Messenian War 736–716	
700		Theopompus 720–675	Tarentum founded 706	Hesiod
	Polydorus 700–665	Anaxandridas I 675–660	First musical contest at Carnea 676	Lelantine War Gyges king of Lydia 685–657
	Eurycrates 665–640	Archidamus I 660–645	Defeat by Argos at Hysiae 669	Pheidon king at Argos 680–655
650				Cypselus tyrant at Corinth 657–625
	Anaxandros 640–615	Anaxilas 645–625	Second Messenian War 640–620	Samian voyage to Tartessus 638
				Cyrene founded 630
600	Eurycratidas 615–590	Leotychidas I 625–600		Peisander tyrant at Corinth 625–585
				Foundation of Naucratis 610
				Foundation of Massilia 600
575	Leon 590–560			Solon's reforms at Athens 594
		Hippocratidas 600–575		Siege of Tyre by Assyrians 586
				Tyrants expelled from Corinth 580
	Anaxandridas II 560–520	Agesicles 575–550	Wars with Tegea 575–50	Amasis king of Egypt 570–526
			Chilon ephor 556	Croesus king of Lydia 560–546
550			Beginning of Pelopon-nesian League 550	Fall of Sardis 546
525		Ariston 550–515	Embassy from Croesus 550	Polycrates tyrant of Samos 540–522
			Battle of Thyrea 546	

BC	*Kings of Sparta*		*Spartan History*	*External Events*
500			Samian expedition 525	Persian conquest of Egypt 525
	Cleomenes I 520–490		Cleomenes in Boeotia 519	Hippias expelled from Athens 510
		Demaratus 515–491	Embassy of Maeandrius 515	Reforms of Cleisthenes 507
			Cleomenes at Athens 508	
475	Leonidas I 490–480		Embassy of Aristagoras 499	Ionian revolt 499–493
		Leotychidas II 491–469	Battle of Sepeia 494	Battle of Marathon 490
			Battle of Thermopylae 480	Battle of Salamis 480
	Pleistarchus 480–459		Battle of Plataea 479	Confederacy of Delos 478
			Recall of Pausanias 478	
450	Pleistoanax 459–409	Archidamus I 469–427	Death of Pausanias 471	Battle of Eurymedon 468
			Earthquake and helot revolt 464	Rise of Pericles 461
			Battle of Tanagra 457	Treasury of Delian League transferred to Athens 454
			War with Athens 457–445	
			Peloponnesian War begins 431	
425		Agis II 427–399	Surrender at Sphacteria 425	
			Brasidas in Thrace 424–422	
400			Peace of Nicias 421	
			Occupation of Decalea 413	Sicilian expedition 415–413
	Pausanias 409–395		Alliance with Persia 412	
			Fall of Athens 404	
375		Agesilaus II 399–360		Expedition of Ten Thousand 401–399
	Agesipolis I 395–380			Revolt of Thebes 379
	Cleombrotus 380–371			Second Athenian League 377
350	Agesipolis II 371–370		Battle of Leuctra 371	
			Liberation of Messenia 370	
	Cleomenes II 370–309		Laconia invaded 369	
			Megalopolis founded 368	
		Archidamus III 360–338	Battle of Mantinea 362	Death of Epaminondas 362

NOTES: Dates before about 550 are approximate. The dates given for the Spartan kings are those suggested by Forrest, 21–2.

Notes

Abbreviations

AA	*Archäologischer Anzeiger*
AJA	*American Journal of Archaeology*
AO	*The Sanctuary of Artemis Orthia,* ed. R. M. Dawkins
AR	*Archaeological Reports*
Arch. Delt.	*Arkhaioloyikon Deltion*
Ath. Mitt.	*Mitteilungen des deutschen archäologischen Instituts, Athenische Abteilung*
BCH	*Bulletin de Correspondance Hellénique*
BSA	*Annual of the British School at Athens*
CAH	*Cambridge Ancient History*
CQ	*Classical Quarterly*
CR	*Classical Review*
DAI	Deutsches Archäologisches Institut, Athens
Ergon	*Greek Archaeological Society, To Ergon*
FGrH	*Fragmente der griechischen Historiker,* ed. F. Jacoby
GIT	*Greek-Illyrian Treasures from Yugoslavia* (1974)
Harv. Stud.	*Harvard Studies in Classical Philology*
IG	*Inscriptiones Graecae.*
JDAI	*Jahrbuch des deutschen archäologischen Instituts*
JHS	*Journal of Hellenic Studies*
JOAI	*Jahreshefte des Österreichischen archäologischen Instituts in Wien*
OCT	Oxford Classical Texts
Ol. Ber.	*Berichte über die Ausgrabungen in Olympia* (DAI).
Page, *Epigr. Gr.*	D. L. Page, *Epigrammata Graeca* (1975)
Page, *PMG*	D. L. Page, *Poetae Melici Graeci* (1962).
Perachora	H. Payne and T. J. Dunbabin, *Perachora: the Sanctuaries of Hera Akraia and Limenia,* 2 v. (1940–62)
POxy.	*Oxyrhynchus Papyri*
PW	A. Pauly, G. Wissowa and W. Kroll, *Real-Encyclopädie der klassischen Altertumswissenschaft*
REA	*Revue des études anciennes*
REG	*Revue des études grecques*
SEG	*Supplementum Epigraphicum Graecum*
TW	M. N. Tod and A. J. B. Wace, *A Catalogue of the Sparta Museum* (1906).

Books listed in the bibliography are referred to by the surname of the author, or by author and short title if more than one book by the same author is listed. Ancient authors are referred to by the customary abbreviations, e.g. Herod., Thuc.

In references large roman numerals denote volumes, small roman numerals plates, and arabic numerals pages, unless otherwise indicated.

Titles in modern Greek are given in the English or French form used for the summary, if there is one; otherwise they are translated into English followed by [in Greek].

Chapter 1

1 Plato, *Laws*, 666d.
2 Thucydides, *The Peloponnesian War*, I, 10.
3 K. G. Feidler, *Reise durch . . . Griechenland* (Leipzig, 1840), I, 321.
4 W. M. Leake, *Travels in the Morea* (London, 1830), I, 157–60.
5 H. Dressel and A. Milchhöfer, *Ath. Mitt.* II (1877), 293–474.
6 J. P. Mahaffy, *Rambles and Studies in Greece* (4th edn, London, 1892), 393–4.
7 J. C. F. Manso, *Sparta: ein Versuch zur Aufklärung der Geschichte und Verfassung dieses Staates* (3v., Leipzig, 1800–5). The library of the British School at Athens has over forty dissertations and pamphlets on Sparta published before 1910, collected by M. N. Tod.
8 For books and articles referred to in the rest of this chapter, see the bibliography pp. 171–75.
9 The custom by which selected young men were sent out into the remote parts of the country to live roughly and, at least after 464, to intimidate the helots.

Chapter 3

1 The Mycenaean sites are described by H. Waterhouse and R. Hope Simpson in *BSA* LV (1960), 67–108 and LVI (1961), 114–175. The evidence for

depopulation is discussed by Desborough, *Last Mycenaeans*, 88–90 and Snodgrass, 363–7.
2 This account of Laconian III is largely based on the material catalogued by Stibbe.
3 *Ergon*, 1960, 168.
4 Now published by Stibbe in *Medelingen Nederlands Inst.*, Rome, XXXVIII (1976), v, 1. I owe this reference to Mr John Boardman.
5 Charmian Clift, *Mermaid Singing* (London, 1958), 192–3. On these vases generally see A. Seeberg, *Corinthian Komos Vases* (London, 1971).
6 Herod. II, 167. There is a good discussion of the supposed monopoly of trade and industry by the *perioeci* by R. T. Ridley in *Mnemosyne*, series 4, XXVII, 281–92.

Chapter 4

1 Christou's date for the beginning of the series may be too early. The style looks not much earlier than Laconian III.
2 P. Leigh Fermor, *Mani: travels in the southern Peloponnese* (London, 1958), 24. For a good account of the making of large jars in modern Crete, see S. Xanthoudides in *Essays in Aegean Archaeology presented to Sir Arthur Evans*, ed. S. Casson, Oxford 1927, 124–5, xx–xxi.

Chapter 5

1 The peasant is on Cambridge, Fitzwilliam Museum GR 133.1923. There is a drawing in *AO*, clv, 1.

Chapter 6

1 E. g. Paus. V, xvii, 1–3 (Dorycleidas, Theocles and Medon); xxiii, 7 (Ariston and Telestas); VI, ix, 8 (Theocles), 14 (Dontas).
2 Sparta Mus. 1005; good illustration in Steinhauer, 57.
3 Sparta Mus. Yeraki 2, ill. *BSA* XI (1904–5), 101.
4 Athens NM 3120, ill. BSA XI, iii.
5 Th. Karagiorga, *Arch. Delt.* XIX A′ (1964), 121, no 28.
6 A. Delivorrias, *Arch. Delt.* XXIV B′ (1969), 131–2 cxx-cxxi.

Chapter 7

1 The figure from the Alpheus valley is in Baltimore, Walters Art Gallery 54.789; Mitten and Doeringer no 9. A similar but smaller figure on a bronze lid from Macedonia (Belgrade NM 13216; *GIT* no 171) is described as 'Macedonian Hallstatt'. D. L. Popovic calls the fine blacksmith from Vranests (Belgrade NM 999/1; *GIT* no 170) 'Peloponnesian'. Lucy Curtis Turnbull, in a thesis which I have not seen, suggests a Tegean origin for these bronzes (Harv. Stud. LXV (1961), 273).
The ivory figure is AO clxix, 3.
2 J. Bouzek, 'Openwork "bird-cage" bronzes' in *The European Community in Later Prehistory*, ed. J. Boardman, M. A. Brown and T. G. E. Powell (London, 1971), 56–76.
3 On these see P. Cartledge 'Early Sparta', 167–84.
4 Pausanias III, xvi, 5.
5 Sparta Mus. 2017; Lamb xxviic.
6 Sparta Mus. 2022.
7 J. D. Beazley, *Potter and Painter in Ancient Athens* (London, 1946), 7.
8 R. Hampe, *Ol. Ber.* I, 77; Beazley, l.c.
9 Athens NM 7465.
10 The votive statuettes are Athens NM 5897 and 15900; Paris, Louvre 138; Vienna Kunst. Mus. 4979. Mirror handles known to me are: Athens NM 6631, 7540 7548, 13975; Belgrade NM 825/1; Berlin St. Mus. 10820, 31084; Leningrad, Hermitage, Mus.; Munich Mus. Ant. Kleinkunst 3452; New York Metr. Mus. 06:1104, 38.11.3, CB 447; Paris, Louvre n.n.; Sparta Mus. 594, 3302; Syracuse Mus.; Vienna Kunst. Mus. 2925.
11 The principal dissentients are Richter, *AJA* XLII (1938), 337–44, and Häfner. Richter finds these 'slim little girls' not the 'muscular athletes' she expects Spartan women to be, but 'dainty dancing girls'. She believes they are *hetaerae*, and therefore Corinthian. Häfner distinguishes three groups, attributed respectively to Laconia, other parts of Greece, and Etruria.
12 Athens NM 7598; Lamb xxviiia.
13 Athens NM 7644; Zervos 242.
14 Ath. XV 678b; *FGrH* fr. 5. On the crowns, see E. Kunze *Ol. Ber* V, 98.
15 Athens NM 6174; Zervos, 215.
16 Pesaro. Mus. Oliv. 3314–5; H. Jucker, *Antike Kunst* VII (1964), i, 1, ii, 1.
17 Paus, V. xxiii, 7. The hydria is in Mainz, Akad. Arch. Mus. 201; Charbonneaux, i, 1.
18 My treatment of the large bronze vessels owes much to the work of Brian Shefton of the University of Newcastle on Tyne, which he very kindly discussed with me in 1975.
19 VIIIe Congrès International d'Archéologie Classique, Paris, 1963. *Le rayonnement des civilisations*, 386–90.
20 Herod. I, 70.
21 Belgrade NM 173/1; *GIT* vi. Berlin St. Mus. Fr 768; Charbonneaux ii, 1.
22 *AA* 1933, 479 fig. 19–20.
23 H. Lechat, *La sculpture attique avant Pheidias* (Paris, 1904), 379.

Chapter 8

1 The first is *IG* V, i, 1; R. Meiggs and D. M. Lewis, *A Selection of Greek Historical Inscriptions*, Oxford, 1969, no. 67. The second, first published in 1974, is discussed in *Liverpool Classical Monthly* I (1976), 87–92 (P. Cartledge) and III (1978), 133–41 (D. H. Kelly) and 189–90 (Cartledge). It is referred to by Cartledge in *JHS* XCVIII (1978), 35, where also the inscriptions from outside Laconia are conveniently listed.
2 H. W. Catling and H. Cavanagh, 'Two inscribed bronzes from the Menelaion' (*Kadmos* XV, 1976, 145–57); Cartledge, *JHS* XCVIII, 1978, 25–6.
3 *AO*, 367 no. 169, 5.

4 *BSA* XXIV (1919–24), 137; Jeffery no. 43.
5 Sparta Mus. 440; *IG* V, i, 213; Jeffery no. 52. Text and commentary in C. D. Buck, *The Greek Dialects* (Chicago, 1955), no. 71.
6 *IG*V, i, 1228–32; Jeffery nos 53–4; Buck nos 72–3.
7 Bowl, *IG* V, i, 1563; Jeffery no. 10. Seat, *SEG* XI, 1180a; Jeffery no. 15. Base, *IG* V, i, 1562; Jeffery no. 49; Meiggs and Lewis no. 22.
8 *AO* 381, fig. 145.

Chapter 9

1 Plato, *Laws*, 629.
2 Callinus, 1, 20–21.
3 Tyrtaeus 11, 3–4, 11–14, 17–34. All references to Tyrtaeus use West's numbering.
4 Tyrtaeus 12.
5 Tyrtaeus 10, 21–5.
6 Tyrtaeus 18–23.
7 Tyrtaeus 2.
8 Tyrtaeus 5.
9 Tyrtaeus 6–7.
10 Herod. VI, 58.
11 Tyrtaeus 4.
12 The distinction is that of Mr John Crook in a letter to the author.
13 *POxy* 2390: Page *PMG* 5.
14 Page 82; Edmonds 28.
15 Page 26; Edmonds 26.
16 Page 89; Edmonds 36.
17 Page 3, 61–81.
18 Page 1; 59b; 4.
19 Page 19; Edmonds 138.
20 Page 17; Edmonds 46.
21 Page 41; Edmonds 62.
22 Page 64; Edmonds 66.
23 Page 95a; Edmonds 73–4.
24 Page 98; Edmonds 87.
25 Page 1; Edmonds 1.
26 For Dionysodotus, Ath. XV, 678b, Edmonds *Lyra Graeca* i, 46; for Spendon, Plut., Lycurgus 28; for Gitiadas, Paus. III, xvii, 2.
27 Ion of Samos, Page, *Epigr. Gr.*, 509.
28 Aristophanes, *Lysistrata*, tr. B. B. Rogers, 1308–15.

Chapter 10

1 Diod. Sic. XI, 11; Page *PMG* 531.
2 Herod. VII, 228; Page *Epigr. Gr.*, 226. By the fourth century *rhemata* (words or orders) had been replaced by *nomima* (customs or laws), e.g. in the speech of the Athenian orator Lycurgus *Against Leocrates*, 109.
3 Herod. VII, 152.
4 Herod. I, 65–70, 82–3, 152–3.
5 Herod. III, 44–7, 54–6, 148.
6 Herod. IV, 145–65.
7 Herod. V, 39–51, 63–4, 70–6, 90–3, 97.
8 Herod. VI, 48–86.
9 Herod. VI, 108; Thuc. III, 68, with Gomme's note.
10 Herod. VI, 106, 120.
11 Herod. VII, 223–4.
12 Herod. VII, 104, 209, 234–5.
13 Herod. IX, 6–11, 19–85.
14 Herod. IX, 90–106.
15 Strabo VIII, v, 5 = *FGrH* IIA, A117; Pindar, *Pythian Odes*, 1, 5.
16 Strabo VI, iii, 2 = *FGrH* IIIB, fr. 13.
17 Thuc. I, 18.
18 Thuc. I, 67–8, 118–25; V, 17–22.
19 Thuc. IV, 80; V, 57.
30 Thuc. V, 66–75.

Chapter 11

1 Aristotle, *Politics*, II, 9.
2 Strabo VIII, v, 4–5 = *FGrH* IIA, fr. 7A.
3 Thuc. V, 19; VIII, 58: II, 2.
4 Plut. *Lycurgus*, 6. The fullest discussion is H. T. Wade-Gery, *CQ* XXXVII–XXXVIII (1943–44) (*Essays in Greek History*, Oxford, 1958, 37–85), the most recent, with select bibliography, R. Sealey, *A History of the Greek States* (Berkeley, 1976), 74–87.

Chapter 12

1 On the Colonnade, Paus. III, xi, 3; Vitruv. I, i, 6. On the Menelaeum, H. W. Catling in *AR* 1976–77, 35–8.
2 Paus. VI, ii, 1.
3 Plut., *Lysander*, 17.
4 Plut., *Lycurgus*, 1.

Select Bibliography

General

1 Books published since 1945

CAVAIGNAC, E., *Sparte*, Paris 1948.
CHRIMES, K. M. T., *Ancient Sparta*, Manchester 1949; 2nd edn, 1952.
FORREST, W. G., *A History of Sparta, 950–192 B.C.*, London 1968.
HUXLEY, G. L., *Early Sparta*, London 1962.
JONES, A. H. M., *Sparta*, Oxford 1967.
KIECHLE, F., *Lakonien und Sparta*, Munich 1963.
MICHELL, H., *Sparta*, Cambridge 1952.
OLIVA, P., *Sparta and her Social Problems*, Prague 1971.
ROUSSEL, P., *Sparte*, Paris 1939; 2nd edn, 1960.
TOYNBEE, A. J., 'The Rise and Decline of Sparta', in *Some Problems of Greek History*, part iii, London 1969.
Of these FORREST is the best short introduction, OLIVA contains the fullest bibliography of earlier literature.

2 Sparta Museum

TOD, M. N. and WACE, A. J. B., *A Catalogue of the Sparta Museum*, n.p. 1906; reprint Rome 1968.
CHRISTOU, CH. A. Ancient Sparta: a short guide to its history, its monuments and its museum [in Greek]. Sparta 1960.
STEINHAUER, G., *Museum of Sparta*, Athens 1976. An excellent illustrated guide.

3 Archaeology

Preliminary reports of the main excavations at Sparta are in *BSA* XII (1905/6) to XVI (1909/10) and XXVI (1923/4) to XXX (1928/9). The final report on the site of the temple of Orthia is *The Sanctuary of Artemis Orthia at Sparta*, ed. R. M. DAWKINS, London 1929 (*AO*). Material from the Menelaeum is collected in *BSA* XV, that from the acropolis in *BSA* XXVIII. The latest excavations at the Menelaeum are briefly reported in *AR* 1976/7 and 1977/8. Trial excavations at Angelona and Yeraki are reported in *BSA* XI (1904/5). Reports of the German excavations at the Amyclaeum are in *Ath. Mitt.* LII (1927), 65–85 by E. BUSCHOR and W. VON MASSOW, and *JDAI* XXXIII (1918), by E. FIECHTER (on the architecture). Christou's excavations at the shrine of Agamemnon and Cassandra at Amyclae are described in *Praktika* 1956, 211–2 and *Ergon* 1956, 100–4; 1960, 167–73; and 1961, 172–4.

CARTLEDGE, P. A., 'Early Sparta c. 950–650: an archaeological and historical study' (D. Phil. Thesis, Oxford 1975), is a very thorough re-examination of the evidence for the early period, including much material in the store of the Sparta Museum not previously used.

Chapter 1

1 The fullest of the old accounts of Spartan institutions, quoting the ancient literary sources, is G. GILBERT *The Constitutional Antiquities of Sparta and Athens*, London 1895 (translated from the second German edn of 1892), 1–91.

2 The Myth

OLLIER, F., *Le mirage spartiate*, 2 v., Paris 1933–43; reprint New York 1974.
The definitive account of the formation of the myth up to Plutarch.
RAWSON, E., *The Spartan Tradition in European Thought*, Oxford 1969.
TIGERSTEDT, E. N., *The Legend of Sparta in Classical Antiquity*, Stockholm 1965. Useful for its references to the modern literature.

3 Reconstruction (in order of publication).

1912 DICKINS, G., 'The Growth of Spartan Policy', *JHS* XXXII, 1–42.
NILSSON, M. P., 'Die Grundlagen des spartischen Lebens', *Klio* XII, 308–40.
1913 JEANMAIRE, H., 'La cryptie lacédémonienne', *REG* XXVI, 121–50.
TOYNBEE, A. J., 'The Growth of Sparta', *JHS* XXXIII, 246–75.
1917 PARETI, L., *Studi di Sparta archaica* I (all published), Florence.
1924 EHRENBERG, V., 'Spartiaten und Lakedaimonier', *Hermes* LIX, 23–73.
1925 EHRENBERG, V., *Neugründer des Staates*, Munich.
GLOTZ, G., 'Sparte jusqu'aux guerres médiques', *Histoire greque*, I, ch. ix, 335–74, Paris.
WADE-GERY, H. T., 'The Growth of the Dorian States', *CAH* III, ch. xxii, 527–70.
1929 EHRENBERG, V., 'Sparta (Geschichte)', *PW* III, 2A, 1373–1453.
1933 KUNZE, E., *Gnomon* IX, 1–14 (review of *Artemis Orthia*).

1935 BLAKEWAY, A., *CR* XLIX, 185–6 (review of Ollier).

1938 ANDREWES, A., 'Eunomia', *CQ* XXXII, 89–102.

JEANMAIRE, H., *Couroi et courètes: essai sur l'éducation spartiate et sur les rites d'adolescence dans l'antiquité hellénique*, Lille.

1950 HAMMOND, N. G. L., 'The Lycurgean Reform at Sparta', *JHS* LXX, 42–64.

STUBBS, H. W., 'Spartan Austerity: a possible explanation', *CQ* XLIV, 32–7.

1954 ANDREWES, A., *Probouleusis: Sparta's contribution to the technique of government*, Oxford.

1956 ANDREWES, A., 'The Spartan Alternative to Tyranny', *The Greek Tyrants*, ch. vi, 66–77, London.

WILL, E., *Doriens et ioniens: essai sur la valeur du critère ethnique appliqué à l'étude d'histoire et de civilisation grecque*, Paris.

1963 BOARDMAN, J., 'Artemis Orthia and Chronology', *BSA* LVIII, 1–7.

1965 JANNI, P., *La cultura di Sparta arcaica: ricerche*, I, Rome.

STARR, C. G., 'The Credibility of early Spartan History', *Historia* XIV, 257–72.

1966 ANDREWES, A., 'The Government of Classical Sparta', *Ancient Society and Institutions: studies presented to Victor Ehrenberg*, 1–20, Oxford.

FORREST, W. G., 'Revolution in Sparta', *The Emergence of Greek Democracy*, ch. v, 123–42, London.

1968 FINLEY, M. I., 'Sparta', *Problèmes de la guerre en Grèce ancienne* ed. VERNANT, J. P., ch. vi, 143–60, Paris.

1970 JANNI, P., *La cultura di Sparta arcaica: ricerche* II, Rome.

1977 HOLLADAY, A. J., 'Spartan Austerity', *CQ* n.s. XXVII, 111–26.

The important group of articles on Sparta in *Ktema* II (1977) came to my notice too late for me to use.

Chapter 2

1 The main ancient source is PAUSANIAS, *Guide to Greece*, III (Laconia), most conveniently consulted in the translation by P. Levi, II, London 1971.

2 Modern Geography

The best and most detailed treatment is A. PHILIPPSON, *Die griechischen Landschaften: eine Landeskunde* III, pt ii (Frankfurt a. Main 1959), 412–508. More general are Great Britain, Admiralty, Naval Intelligence Division, *Greece*, 3 v., London 1944, and J. SION, 'Le Peloponnèse (Morée)', *Géographie universelle*, ed. P. VIDAL DE LA BLACHE and L. GALLOIS, VII, pt ii, ch. xxxix, 548–59, Paris 1934.

3 Topography and routes

LEAKE, W. M., *Travels in the Morea*, 3 v., London 1830, is still basic. The results of a topographical reconnaissance of Laconia by members of the British School were published in *BSA* XIII (1906/7) to XVI (1909/10).

For the country before the advent of modern roads and motor transport the British Admiralty *Handbook of Greece*, London 1918, with detailed descriptions of roads and tracks, is invaluable. Old guide books such as MURRAY'S *Handbook for travellers in Greece*, new edn, London 1854, and BAEDEKER'S *Greece: handbook for travellers*, Leipzig 1905, are also useful.

The best modern guide is the 'Blue Guide' *Greece*, ed. S. ROSSITER, 3rd edn, London 1977.

4 Maps

Good maps of Greece are less rare than they used to be. The British War Office, *Greece*, London 1944, is on a scale of 1:100,000 and shows contours. Sheets L5–8, M5–8 and N7–8 cover Laconia. The best topographical map is that of the National Statistical Service of Greece, *Nomos Lakonias*, 1:200,000, Athens 1963, contoured at 200 metres. Tourist maps showing localities and modern roads are P. D. Coumoutsides *Khartis Lakonias*, 1:200,000, Sparta 1973, and D. and V. Loukopoulos *Morfoloyikos Khartis Peloponnisou*, 1:300,000, Athens, no date but *c.* 1970.

Chapter 3

1 General

COOK, R. M., *Greek Painted Pottery*, 2nd edn, London 1972, is the best introduction, with a concise treatment of the various periods of Laconian vase painting. E. LANE'S pioneer study, 'Lakonian Vase Painters', *BSA* XXXIV (1933/4), 99–198, xx–xl/ix, remains valuable, and has the only full treatment of the period between Geometric and Laconian III. P. PELAGATTI, 'La ceramica laconica del Museo di Taranto', *Annuale della Scuola Archeologica di Atene*, XXXIII (1955/6) is important both for vases published for the first time and for grave contexts.

2 Protogeometric and Geometric

These are covered respectively by V. R. D.'A. DESBOROUGH, *Protogeometric Pottery*, Oxford 1952, and J. N. COLDSTREAM, *Greek Geometric Pottery*, London 1968. On the interval between Mycenaean and Protogeometric see DESBOROUGH, *The Last Mycenaeans and their Successors*, London 1972, 87–90 and A. M. SNODGRASS, *The Dark Ages of Greece*, Edinburgh 1972, 360–402.

3 Laconian III–IV

SHEFTON, B. B., 'Three Laconian Vase Painters', *BSA* XLIX (1954), 299–310, examines 115 vases and divides them between three artists, with their workshops and imitators. This is supplemented by his section on 'Other non-Corinthian Vases', in *Perachora* II, ed. T. J. Dunbabin, Oxford 1962, 369–85.

STIBBE, C. M., *Lakonische Vasenmaler des sechsten Jahrhunderts*, 2 v., Amsterdam 1972, catalogues, attributes and illustrates 370 vases, with a full bibliography. Though sometimes controversial, his conclusions have generally been followed here.

4 Architectural Terracottas

VAN BUREN, E. D., *Greek Fictile Revetments in the Archaic Period*, London 1926, is the basic work, together with *AO* ch. iii (117–44). More recent is H. LAUTER-BUFÉ, 'Entstehung und Entwicklung des combinierten lakonischen Acroters', *Ath. Mitt.* LXXXIX (1974), 205–30.

Chapter 4

1 General

HIGGINS, R. A., *Greek Terracottas*, London 1967. Publication of Laconian terracottas must for the most part be sought out in the excavation reports, especially in *AO*, *BSA* XIV, XV and XXVIII and *Ergon* 1956, 1960 and 1961.

2 Daedalic

JENKINS, R. H., 'Laconian Terracottas of the Daedalic Style', *BSA* XXXIII (1932/3), 66–79.

3 Relief Jars

CHRISTOU, CH. A., 'The new amphora from Sparta: the other amphorae with reliefs of Laconian manufacture' [in Greek, English summary], *Arch. Delt.* XIX A′ (1964), 164–265, 285–7, is a full discussion with a catalogue of all known fragments.

4 The Masks

BSA XII, 338–43 (R. C. BOSANQUET); *AO* ch. v, 163–86 (G. DICKINS).

Chapter 5

1 General

MARANGOU, E.-L., *Lakonische Elfenbein- und Beinschnitzereien*, Tübingen 1969, is a model work, well illustrated and splendidly documented.

2 Eastern Influences

R. D. BARNETT discusses the influence of oriental art on the Spartan ivories in 'Early Greek and Oriental Ivories', *JHS* LXVIII (1948), 1–25, and in 'Oriental Influences on Archaic Greece', *The Aegean and the Near East: studies presented to Hetty Goldman*, ed. S. WEINBERG, New York 1956, 212–38. There is useful material in T. J. DUNBABIN, *The Greeks and their Eastern Neighbours*, London 1957. J. NIZETTE-GODFROID, 'Contribution à l'étude de l'influence du lion néo-Hittite sur la constitution du type léonin dans l'art grec orientalisant', *Antiquité Classique* XLI (1972), 5–48, discusses the various types of lion in Archaic Greek art.

For Asian predecessors of the Greek ivories see Sir M. MALLOWAN, *The Nimrud Ivories*, London 1978. The best account of the Phoenicians is D. B. HARDEN, *The Phoenicians*, London 1962 (2nd edn, 1972).

Chapter 6

1 General

There is no satisfactory study of Laconian sculpture as a whole. For the early finds WACE's survey, TW 99–131, is still useful. Since the excavations there have been two systematic studies, both covering bronzes as well as sculpture in stone. E. LANGLOTZ in *Frühgriechische Bilderhauerschulen*, Nuremberg 1927, was the first to attempt a comprehensive definition and list; his Laconian school has stood the test of time better than some of his others. U. HÄFNER, in *Das Kunstschaffen Laconiens*, (Diss. Münster 1965), considerably extends Langlotz's catalogue, but is too sceptical of attributions to Laconia and too low in many of her dates. Stimulating short accounts are G. KARO, *Greek Personality in Archaic Sculpture*, Cambridge, Mass., 1948, 143–68, and E. HOMANN-WEDEKING, 'Von spartanischer Art und Kunst', *Antike und Abendland* VII (1958), 63–72.

2 Fonts

J. DUCAT, 'Perirrhanteria', *BCH* LXXXVIII (1964), argues for the Laconian origin of the series. A. DELIVORRIAS, 'Laconian Perirrhanteria' [in Greek, English summary], *Athens Annals of Archaeology* II (1969), 7–10 discusses the base from Sparta. F. W. HAMDORF 'Lakonische Perirrhanteria', *Ath. Mitt.* LXXXVII (1964), 47–64, is cautious. The series, except those from Sparta and the Amyclaeum, is well shown in G. RICHTER, *Korai*, London, 1968.

3 Seated Figures

KRANZ, P., 'Frühe griechische Sitzfiguren', *Ath. Mitt.* LXXXVII (1972), 1–55.

4 Hero Reliefs

ANDRONIKOS, M., 'Laconian Reliefs' [in Greek], *Peloponnesiaka* I (1956), 254–314.

Chapter 7

1 General

The best introductions are W. LAMB, *Greek and Roman Bronzes*, London 1929 (reprint Chicago, 1969); J. CHARBONNEAUX, *Les bronzes grecs*, Paris 1958 (English translation, London 1962); and D. G. MITTEN and S. DOERINGER, *Bronzes from the Classical World*, Boston, Mass. 1967. C. ROLLEY, *Die Bronzen* (Monumenta Graeca et Romana V, fasc. i), Leiden, 1967, is a useful selection of pictures and C. ZERVOS, *L'art en Grèce*, 2nd edn, Paris 1936, contains good illustrations of a number of Laconian bronzes. For comparison, K. WALLENSTEIN, *Korinthische Plastik des 7. und 6. Jahrhunderts vor Christus*, Bonn 1971, is especially useful.

Essential information is scattered through periodicals and museum catalogues, notably in the successive contributions of Kunze to *Ol. Ber.* Only a few of the more important items directly related to topics discussed in the text can be listed.

2 Mirror Stands

First discussed by C. PRASCHNIKER, 'Bronzener Spiegelstütze im Wiener Hofmuseum', *JÖAI* XV (1912), 219–52, and later by K. SCHEFOLD, 'Griechischer Spiegel', *Die Antike* XVI (1940), 11–37' The best treatment is now TH. KARAGIORGA, 'Un miroir laconien au musée de Sparte' [in Greek, French summary], *Arch. Delt.* XX A′ (1965), 96–109.

3 Hoplite Statuettes

The fullest discussions are H. Bloesch, 'Spartanische Krieger', *Museum Helveticum* XVI (1959), 249–56, and most recently M. Jost, 'Statuettes de bronze de Lykosoura', *BCH* XCIX (1975), 355–63.

4 Standing Youths

This type is discussed by Ch. Karusou, 'Ein lakonischer Apollon', *Charites* ed. K. Schauenburg, Bonn 1957, 33–7; by E. Kunze, 'Ein Bronzejüngling', *Ol. Ber.* V (1941–52), 97–102; and, most recently, by C. Leon, 'Statuette eines Kuros aus Messenien', *Ath. Mitt.* LXXXIII (1968), 175–85.

5 Large Vessels

The water-jars are catalogued by E. Diehl, *Die Hydria*, Mainz 1964; the Telestas vase is discussed by G. Häfner in *Charites*, 118–26. The Vix bowl was published and similar bowls listed by R. Joffroy, *Monuments Piot* XLVIII (1954), 1–68, and in more popular style in his *Le trésor de Vix*, Paris 1962. Amont those who argue for its Laconian origin are A. Rumpf, 'Krater lakonikos', *Charites*, 127–35, and U. Gehrig, 'Der Krater lakonikos', *AA* 1971, 602–12; against, G. Vallet and F. Villard, 'Un atelier de bronziers: sur l'école du cratère de Vix', *BCH* LXXIX (1955), 50–74, (South Italy) and M. Gjordesen, 'Greek Bronzes: a review article', *AJA* LXVII (1963), 333–51 (Corinth). For the Trebenište finds, see L. Popovic, *Katalog Nalaza iz Nekropole kod Trebenište* [Serbo Croat and French], Belgrade, 1956, and *GIT*. Gorgons are studied by Th. Karagiorga, 'Gorgoneia laconiens', [in Greek, French summary], *Arch. Delt.* XIX A′ (1964), 116–22.

6 Attached Ornaments

D. E. L. Haynes, 'A Bronze Banqueter', *British Museum Quarterly* XX (1955), 36–7, and E. Kunze, 'Archaische Silene', *Ol. Ber.* VIII 236–50, deal respectively with banqueters and silens.

Chapter 8

1 The miscellaneous objects from the Orthia site were published in *AO* ch. xi, 378–98.

2 Lead Figurines

The classification by A. J. B. Wace in TW, 228–9 is still useful. Wace also published the finds from the Menelaeum, *BSA* XV (1908/9), 127–41, and from the Orthia site, *AO* ch ix, 249–84.

3 Inscriptions

Inscriptions from Laconia are collected in *IG* V, i, Berlin 1913, supplemented by *BSA* XXIV (1919–21), 88–143, and *SEG* I to date. Most are of the Roman period. A useful selection of the earlier inscriptions is in L. H. Jeffery, *Local Scripts of Archaic Greece*, Oxford 1961, 198–202. P. A. Cartledge considers the epigraphical evidence in 'Literacy in the Spartan Oligarchy', *JHS* XCVIII, 1978, 25–37.

Chapter 9

1 Tyrtaeus

Text: *Iambi et Elegi Graeci*, ed. M. L. West, II, Oxford 1972.
Text and translation: *Elegy and Iambus*, ed. J. M. Edmonds, I., London 1931 (Loeb Classical Library).
Text and commentary: *Early Greek Elegy*, ed. T. Hudson Williams, Cardiff, 1926.
Discussion: C. M. Bowra, *Early Greek Elegists*, Cambridge 1935; 2nd edn, 1960, 37–60. W. Jaeger, 'Tyrtaios über die wahre arete', *Sitzungberichte der Preussischen Akademie: Philosophisch-historische Klasse*, 1932, 537–68; reprinted in his *Scripta Minora*, Rome 1960. B. Snell, *Tyrtaios und die Sprache des Epos*, Göttingen 1969. On the adoption of hoplite tactics see especially P. Cartledge, 'Hoplites and Heroes: Sparta's contribution to the technique of ancient warfare', *JHS* XCVII (1977), 11–27. The evidence is most fully set out by A. M. Snodgrass, *Early Greek Armour and Weapons*, Edinburgh 1964, and in more popular form in his *Arms and Armour of the Greeks*, London 1967.

2 Alcman

Text: *Poetae Melici Graeci*, ed. D. L. Page, Oxford 1962.
Text and translation: *Lyra Graeca*, ed. J. M. Edmonds, I, London 1932 (Loeb Classical Library).
Text and commentary (selection): *Greek Melic Poets*, ed. H. W. Smyth, London 1904.
The 'Chorus for Maidens': *The Partheneion*, ed. D. L. Page, Oxford 1951 (text, translation and commentary).
Discussion: C. M. Bowra, *Greek Lyric Poetry*, Oxford 1936; 2nd edn, 1961, 16–76. P. Ianni, *La cultura di Sparta arcaica* I, Rome 1965, 43–120. G. Viansino, 'Notes sur Alcman', *REA* LXXVI (1974), 223–36.

Chapter 10

The text of Simonides's odes is in Page, *PMG*, of the epigrams in Page, *Epigr. Graec.*; for his career, Bowra, *Greek Lyric Poetry*, 317–401.
The text of Herodotus used is that of C. Hude, 2nd edn, Oxford 1912 (OCT), of Thucydides that of H. S. Jones revised by J. Enoch Powell, Oxford 1942 (OCT). Convenient translations of Herodotus are those of G. Rawlinson (Everyman's Library), H. Carter (World's Classics) and A. de Selincourt (Penguin Classics), of Thucydides, those of R. Crawley (Everyman) and R. Warner (Penguin).
Important discussions of fifth-century Sparta are contained in A. W. Gomme, A. Andrewes and K. J. Dover, *A Historical Commentary on Thucydides*, I–IV, Oxford 1945–70 and in G. E. M. de Ste Croix, *The Origins of the Peloponnesian War*, London 1972.

Chapter 11

1 Xenophon

The text of the *Hellenica* is edited by E. C. Marchant, Oxford 1901 (OCT); text and translation by

C. L. Brownson, 2 v., London 1918–21 (Loeb); translation by R. Warner, London 1967 (Penguin). The text of the *Constitution of the Lacedaemonians* is in v. 5 of Marchant's edition of Xenophon's works, Oxford 1920 (OCT); text and translation by Marchant in the Loeb edition v. 7 (London 1925); translation and notes by J. M. Moore in *Aristotle and Xenophon on Democracy and Oligarchy*, London 1975.

2 Aristotle

The text of the *Politics* is edited by D. Ross, Oxford 1957 (OCT); texts and translation by H. Rackham, London 1932 (Loeb); translations by J. Warrington, London 1959 (Everyman), and E. A. Sinclair, London 1969 (Penguin).

3 Plutarch

Text and translation of the *Lives* by B. Perrin, 11 v., London 1914–26 (Loeb); translation by Dryden revised by A. H. Clough, 3 v., London 1910 (Everyman).

4 Pausanias

Text and translation by W. S. Jones and H. A. Ormerod, London 1926 (Loeb); most conveniently consulted in the translation, with notes by P. Levi, 1971 (Penguin).

5 Other authors

Fragments are quoted from *FGrH*. For discussion of later writers on Sparta, see the books by Ollier and Tigerstedt listed above (ch. I, 1). Ancient texts on Sparta are listed by A. H. M. Jones, *Sparta*, 176–82.

List of Illustrations

1 View of Sparta and Taygetus. Photo Hellenic Society.
2 Map of the Vale of Sparta, drawn by Cangraphics Pty Ltd, Canberra, based on Great Britain, War Office, *Greece, 1 : 100,000* (1944), with additions.
3 Diagram, drawn by Cangraphics Pty Ltd, after Vidal de la Blanche and Gallois, *Géographie Universelle* vii pt i, fig. 146.
4 View of the Menelaeum. Photo Hellenic Society.
5 Site of the temple of Orthia. Photo Hannibal.
6 View of Langadha Pass. Photo Hellenic Society.
7 Map of the southern Peloponnese, drawn by Canagraphics Pty Ltd, after Philippson, *Griechische Landschaften* iii, pt ii (1952) and other sources.
8 Athens, NM 234. Trinket box from Amyclae. Drawing by Christine Grishin, after Coldstream, xlvi n.
9 Sparta Mus. Pottery fragment from Amyclae. Drawing by Christine Grishin.
10 Sparta Mus. Pottery fragments from the Amyclaeum. Drawing by Christine Grishin.
11 Sparta Mus. 2954. Pottery fragment from the acropolis. Drawing by Christine Grishin, after Lane, *BSA* xxxiv, xxiii j.
12 Sparta Mus. Pottery fragment from the Menelaeum. Drawing by Christine Grishin, after Lane, *BSA* xxxiv, xxvi a.
13 Taranto, Mus. Naz. 1G 4805. Cup from Tarentum.
14 Map showing distribution of Laconian pottery and bronzes, drawn by Canagraphics Pty Ltd from data supplied by the author.
15 Paris, Bibl. Nat. (Cab. des Médailles) 189. Cup from Vulci.
16 Rome, Vatican Mus. Gregoriano Etrusco 16592. Cup from Caere. Photo Alinari.
17 Paris, Louvre E668 (Campana collection). Cup from Etruria.
18 Paris, Louvre E664 (Campana collection). Wine cup from Etruria. Photo Giraudon.
19 London, BM, B2. Cup from Capua. Drawing by Christine Grishin, after Lane, *BSA* xxxiv, xli c.
20 Paris, Bibl. Nat. (Cab. des Médailles) 190. Cup from Nola.
21 London, BM, B1. Cup, find-site unknown.
22 London, BM, B3. Cup from Sicyon.
23 Paris, Louvre E669 (Campana collection). Cup from Etruria.
24 Paris Louvre E662 (Campana collection). Bowl from Caere.
25 Paris, Louvre E670 (Campana collection). Cup from Etruria.
26 Berlin, Staat. Mus. 3404. Cup from Tarquinia.
27 Paris, Bibl. Nat. (Cab. des Médailles) 192. Cup, find-site unknown.
28 Taranto, Mus. Naz. 52847. Cup from Tarentum.
29 Bonn, Akad. Mus. 62 h. Fragment of bowl from Tarquinia.
30 Basle, Antik. Mus Cup, findsite unknown.
31 Athens, NM 4381. Terracotta head from Amyclae. Photo DAI.
32 Sparta Mus. 1238. Terracotta vase from the temple of Orthia. Photo DAI.
33 Sparta Mus. 3100. Terracotta mould-made head from the acropolis. Photo DAI.
34 Sparta Mus. Terracotta relief head from the temple of Orthia. Photo DAI.
35 Sparta Mus. Three terracotta figures from the temple of Orthia. Photo DAI.
36 Sparta Mus. Terracotta head from the temple of Orthia. Photo DAI.
37 Sparta Mus. Terracotta statuette from the temple of Orthia. Photo DAI.

38 Sparta Mus. Terracotta figurine from the temple of Orthia. Drawing by Christine Grishin, after *AO* xxxiii, 8.

39 Sparta Mus. Terracotta pendant from the temple of Orthia. Drawing by Christine Grishin, after *AO* xxxii, 5.

40 Sparta Mus. Terracotta scent jar from the temple of Orthia. Drawing by Christine Grishin, after *AO* xliii, 4.

41 Sparta Mus. 5395. Terracotta mixing bowl from Sparta. Photo Greek Service of Antiquities.

42 Sparta Mus. Terracotta mask from the temple of Orthia. Photo DIA.

43 Sparta Mus. Terracotta mask from the temple of Orthia. Photo DAI.

44 Sparta Mus. Terracotta mask from the temple of Orthia. Photo DAI.

45 Athens, NM 15505, 15505a, 15511. Ivory brooch-plates from the temple of Orthia. Photo DAI.

46 Athens, NM 15503. Ivory brooch-plate from the temple of Orthia. Photo DAI.

47 Athens, NM 15543. Ivory 'seal' from the temple of Orthia. Photo DAI.

48 Athens, NM 15534. Ivory 'seal' from the temple of Orthia. Photo DAI.

49 Athens, NM 15535. Ivory 'seal' from the temple of Orthia. Photo DAI.

50 Athens, NM 15536. Ivory 'seal' from the temple of Orthia. Photo DAI.

51 Athens, NM 15623. Ivory 'seal' from the temple of Orthia. Photo DAI.

52 Athens, NM 15621. Ivory 'seal' (base) from the temple of Orthia. Photo DAI.

53 Athens, NM. Ivory 'seal' (base) from the temple of Orthia. Drawing by Christine Grishin.

54 Athens, NM. Ivory 'seal' from the temple of Orthia. Drawing by Christine Grishin.

55 Athens, NM. Ivory 'seal' (base) from the temple of Orthia. Drawing by Christine Grishin.

56 Athens, NM. Ivory 'seal' (base) from the temple of Orthia. Drawing by Christine Grishin.

57 Athens, NM 15366. Ivory silhouette from the temple of Orthia. Photo DAI.

58 Athens, NM 15506. Ivory relief plate, perhaps from a box, from the temple of Orthia. Photo DAI.

59 Athens, NM 15509, 15501, 15508. Ivory brooch-plates from the temple of Orthia. Photo DAI.

60 Athens, NM 15520. Ivory plate, perhaps from a box, from the temple of Orthia.

61 Athens, NM 15484. Ivory group from the temple of Orthia. Photo DAI.

62 Athens, NM 15495. Ivory group from the temple of Orthia. Photo DAI.

63 Athens, NM 15792. Ivory relief, perhaps a harness ornament, from the temple of Orthia.

64 Athens, NM 15355. Ivory brooch-plate from the temple of Orthia. Photo DAI.

65 Athens, NM 15525. Ivory comb from the temple of Orthia.

66 Athens, NM 15524. Ivory comb from the temple of Orthia. Drawing by Christine Grishin.

67 Athens, NM 15368. Ivory comb from the temple of Orthia.

68 Athens, NM 15362. Ivory relief from the temple of Orthia. Photo DAI.

69 Sparta Mus. Ivory cup from the temple of Orthia. Photo DAI.

70 Athens, NM 15363. Ivory relief from the temple of Orthia. Photo DAI.

71 Athens, NM 15631. Impression from a bone seal from the temple of Orthia. Photo DAI.

72 Athens, NM 15337a. Bone silhouette from the temple of Orthia. Drawing by Christine Grishin.

73 Athens, NM 15351. Bone ornament for furniture from the temple of Orthia. Drawing by Christine Grishin.

74 Athens, NM 15357. Pair of bronze ornaments, perhaps for a box, from the temple of Orthia.

75 Athens, NM 15338. Bone relief from the temple of Orthia. Photo DAI.

76 Athens, NM 15332. Bone relief from the temple of Orthia. Photo DAI.

77 Athens, NM. Bone ornament for furniture from the temple of Orthia. Drawing by Christine Grishin.

78 Athens, NM. Bone seal (base) from the temple of Orthia. Drawing by Christine Grishin.

79 Sparta Mus. 3362. Relief on slab of blue-grey limestone from Mistra. Photo DAI.

80 Corinth, Isthmia Mus. IS 161. Font from Isthmia. Drawing by Christine Grishin, after *Hesperia* XXVII, viii-ix.

81 Olympia Mus. 26. Font-support in bluish limestone from the temple of Hera at Olympia. Photo DAI.

82 Sparta Mus. 1423. Relief in grey-blue limestone from the base of a font, from Sparta. Photo DAI.

83 Olympia Mus. 1. Head in grey limestone from the temple of Hera at Olympia. Photo Max Hirmer.

84 Sparta Mus. Relief on soft limestone from the temple of Orthia. Drawing by Christine Grishin, after *AO* lxv, 16.

85 Sparta Mus. Relief on soft limestone from the temple of Orthia. Drawing by Christine Grishin, after *AO* lxiv, 12.

86 Sparta Mus. Incised drawing on soft limestone from the temple of Orthia. Drawing by Christine Grishin, after *AO* lxxi, 57.

87 Sparta Mus. Relief on soft limestone from the temple of Orthia. Drawing by Christine Grishin, after Hellenic Society photo.

88 Sparta Mus. Silhouette and relief in soft limestone from the temple of Orthia. Drawing by Christine Grishin, after Hellenic Society photo.

89 Sparta Mus. 1. Relief on four-sided block of bluish-grey marble, from Magoula (Sparta). Photo Hannibal.

90 Reverse of four-sided block. Photo Hannibal.

91 Sparta Mus. 1030. Relief on grey limestone slab from the acropolis. Photo Hannibal.

92 Sparta Mus. 5380. Relief on grey marble slab from Sparta. Photo Hannibal.

93 Sparta Mus. 575. Relief on blue marble slab from Sparta. Photo Hannibal.

94 Berlin, Staat. Mus. 731. Relief on blue-grey marble slab from Khrisafa.
95 Sparta Mus. 4. Relief on bluish marble slab from Sparta. Drawing by Christine Grishin, after Steinhauer, *Museum of Sparta*, fig. 42.
96 Berlin, Staat. Mus. 732. Relief on blue-grey marble slab from Magoula (Sparta).
97 Brussels, Mus. Cinquantenaire A1150. Relief on marble slab from Greece.
98 Sparta Mus. Yeraki 1. Relief on bluish marble slab from Yeraki. Photo DAI.
99 Copenhagen, Ny Carlsberg Glyptotek 423. Relief on blue-grey marble slab.
100 Sparta Mus. Kharuda 1. Relief on white marble slab from Kharuda. Drawing by Christine Grishin.
101 Sparta Mus. 5. Relief on grey limestone slab from Sparta. Drawing by Christine Grishin.
102 Sparta Mus. 654. Relief on blue marble for gable, from Sparta. Drawing by Christine Grishin, after *Arch. Delt.* XIX A', lxxii j.
103 Sparta Mus. 364. Statue in bluish marble from Magoula (Sparta). Photo DAI.
104 Sparta Mus. 5195. Statue in blue-grey marble from the Roman theatre. Photo Hannibal.
105 Sparta Mus. 3365. Statue in white marble from near the acropolis. Photo N. Georgiadkas, Sparta.
106 Sparta Mus. 2155 (b), 2163 (e), 1696 (d); n.n. (c, a). Bronze figurines and brooch. Drawing by Christine Grishin, after *AO* lxxvi k, p and m, and *AO* lxxxi.
107 Sparta Mus. Bronze statuette from the temple of Orthia. Drawing by Christine Grishin.
108 Sparta Mus. 2163. Bronze statuette from the temple of Orthia. Drawing by Christine Grishin.
109 Athens, NM. Bronze shoulder pin from the temple of Orthia. Drawing by Christine Grishin, after *AO* lxxxvi.
110 Sparta Mus. 2024. Bronze statuette from the acropolis. Drawing by Christine Grishin.
111 Sparta Mus. 1691. Bronze statuette from the Menelaeum. Photo DAI.
112 Sparta Mus. 2207. Relief mask from hammered bronze sheet. Photo DAI.
113 Sparta Mus. 2142. Bronze brooch from the temple of Orthia. Photo DAI.
114 Sparta Mus. 2150. Bronze ornament from the temple of Orthia. Photo DAI.
115 Athens, NM 16722. Bronze bridle-ornament from Khandrinou, Messenia.
116 Sparta Mus. 2146. Bronze brooch from the temple of Orthia. Drawing by Christine Grishin.
117 Sparta Mus. 2160. Bronze brooch ornament from the temple of Orthia. Photo DAI.
118 Sparta Mus. 2161. Bronze ornament, probably from neck of a large bowl. Photo DAI.
119 Sparta Mus. 3246. Bronze ornament for box, from the acropolis. Drawing by Christine Grishin.
120 Sparta Mus. 1690. Bronze ornaments, probably from the rim of a bowl. Photo DAI.
121 Sparta Mus. 2148 (b). Bronze statuette from the temple of Orthia. Photo DAI.
122 Sparta Mus. 2017. Bronze statuette from the acropolis. Photo DAI.
123 Sparta Mus. 2148 (a). Bronze statuette from the temple of Orthia. Drawing by Christine Grishin.
124 Athens, NM 15890. Bronze statuette from the temple of Orthia. Photo DAI.
125 Sparta Mus. 2022. Bronze statuette from the acropolis. Photo DAI.
126 Athens, NM 7614. Bronze statuette from the shrine of Apollo Hyperte leatas at Feniki. Photo DAI.
127 Olympia Mus. B25. Bronze statuette from Olympia. Photo DAI.
128 Olympia Mus. B5000. Bronze statuette from Olympia. Photo DAI.
129 Berlin, Staat. Mus. 7933. Bronze stand, perhaps for incense burner, said to be from Sparta.
130 Athens, NM 7540. Bronze stand, probably for a basin, from Kinaitha, Arcadia. Drawing by Christine Grishin, after Lamb, *Greek and Roman Bronzes*, xxvii b.
131 Athens, NM 15897. Bronze statuette from the acropolis. Photo DAI.
132 Sparta Mus. 3302. Bronze mirror from Taygetus. Photo DAI.
133 New York, Met. Mus. 1938. 11.3. Bronze mirror, find-site unknown.
134 London, BM 1859-8-1-18. Bronze statuette, find-site unknown but probably central Italy.
135 London, BM 1929-10-16-6. Bronze statuette, said to be from Sparta.
136 Athens, NM 14789. Bronze statuette from Longa, Messenia. Photo DAI.
137 Oxford, Ashmolean Mus. B415. Bronze statuette from Epirus. Drawing by Christine Grishin.
138 Ioannina Mus. 4914 (formerly Athens NM 15174). Bronze statuette from Dodona. Photo DAI.
139 Athens, NM 13056. Bronze statuette from Mt Lycaeum. Drawing by Christine Grishin.
140 Athens, NM 16365. Bronze statuette from Kosmas, central Laconia. Photo DAI.
141 Berne, Hist. Mus. 11620. Bronze water-jar from Grächwil, near Berne (detail).
142 Olympia Mus. B175. Ornament from handle of bronze water-jar, from Olympia. Photo DAI.
143 Châtillon-sur-Seine, Musée de Ville. Bronze mixing bowl from Vix (detail). Photo Giraudon.
144 Detail of frieze on Vix bowl (see Ill. 143). Photo Chambon, Châtillon-sur-Seine.
145 Belgrade, NM 174/1. Bronze mixing bowl and tripod from Trebenište.
146 Athens, NM 7550. Bronze ornament from neck of a mixing bowl, from Edessa. Drawing by Christine Grishin, after *AA* LXXXVI, fig. 121.
147 London, BM 1954-10-18-1. Bronze ornament from a tripod, probably from Dodona.
148 London, BM 208. Bronze ornament from a tripod, from Prizren, Yugoslavia.
149 Athens, NM 7544. Bronze ornament from a tripod, from Amyclae. Photo DAI.
150 Sparta Mus. Lead figurines from the temple of Orthia. Photo Hellenic Society.

Index

Numerals in *italic* refer to illustration numbers